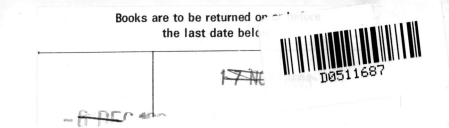

Thirteen **Ways**

Graham Foundation / MIT Press Series in Contemporary
Architectural Discourse

Robert Harbison

13

Thirteen **Ways**

Theoretical Investigations in Architecture

Graham Foundation for Advanced Studies in the Fine Arts Chicago, Illinois

The MIT Press Cambridge, Massachusetts London, England

GF

Publication of this book has been supported by a grant from the Graham Foundation for Advanced Studies in the Fine Arts.

This book was set in Garamond and Meta by The MIT Press and was printed and bound in the United States of America.

Library of Congress Cataloging-in-Publication Data

Harbison, Robert.
    Thirteen ways : theoretical investigations in architecture / Robert Harbison.
        p.   cm. — (Graham Foundation/MIT Press series in contemporary architectural discourse)
    Includes index.
    ISBN 0-262-08256-X (hardcover)
    1. Architecture—Philosophy.   I. Title.   II. Series.
NA2500.H372   1997
720′.1—dc21
                                                        96-44542
                                                            CIP

For John and Artis

Contents

/

This book offers a novel interpretation of what architectural theory might be. Its title refers to two earlier works, a poem and a philosophical treatise, both of unorthodox form. The first is Wallace Stevens's "Thirteen Ways of Looking at a Blackbird," a beautiful example of shattered or oblique structure which approaches its central truth, how sense objects inhabit the world, glancingly in a series of separate forays. It is sometimes hard to tell if the object of the poem, the blackbird, remains the same, because it is given such violent twists in the unseen parts, the spaces between the thirteen fragments.

The poem is much more important than the philosophical work in indicating the intention and character of this book, in which the major tension, the disparity which propels it, the gap across which its energy jumps, is that between the particular and the general, between individual sensory objects and the theoretical ideas they may embody or represent.

The second work referred to in the title is Wittgenstein's *Theoretical Investigations*. This is a joking or at least a more tentative reference than the other, for the present book is conducted from a state of doubt about the very possibility of theory. From this cause flow its most unorthodox properties, first and foremost its apparent formal incoherence. The basis of the book is a series of large themes or concepts, large to begin with and then interpreted extremely freely. The argument moves rapidly between different centuries, between the very large and the noticeably small, between the center and the edge, between buildings and things like them in one or more ways, such as dioramas, paintings, natural formations, or human institutions.

The themes themselves often have a parallel, tangential, or partly overlapping relation to architecture. Moving through them, we follow a broken progress or development from, roughly speaking, the physical to the metaphysical: sculpture, machines, the body, landscape, models, ideas, politics, the sacred, subjectivity, and finally memory. Each time, a well-worn topic is taken up and examined with as few preconceptions as possible, with the aim of a fresh view of its relevance to architecture.

The novelty of the book's procedure can best be illustrated by the detailed sequence of subjects in one of its chapters (here chapter 2, "Machines"). The underlying basis of this chapter is modernism's love affair with machines—as an ideal of impersonal organization and a literal model for art (Le Corbusier's description of a house as a machine for living in)—but its starting point is the Renaissance idea of a machine as an aesthetic device of unusual intricacy: table centerpieces in precious materials, urban pageants, stage scenery, fireworks displays. Elizabethan prodigy houses are then seen as embodying some of these contradictions—war as theater, fortification as decorative excess—and such love of artifice is followed to its culmination in portraits of Elizabeth I as a gorgeous and unapproachable machine. The theme is pursued through Michelangelo's designs for Florentine fortifications, his architecture, and Russian Constructivist liberation of sculpture into pseudo-useful machinery, stage scenery, and then buildings, which culminate in Chernikov's industrial fantasies. These are compared to Shin Takamatsu's science fiction buildings of the 1980s in Japan. Another tradition is traced from the Crystal Palace through Cedric Price and likened to eighteenth-century automata. Now a digression on the stair as a concentration of mechanical intricacy which culminates in Piranesi and the Centre Pompidou in Paris, whose ancestry is traced to Gothic via Viollet-le-Duc, who taught us to see cathedrals as efficient machines. Then a modern designer who builds organisms with machine finishes, Calatrava, leads to the greatest straddler of organism and machine, always seeing one in terms of the other, Leonardo. His dissective approach is seen as the source of some modern ills, and surprisingly as the root idea of a favorite modern institution, the museum. Finally this phase is summed up in the work of one of the most entertaining modernist dissectors, Gerrit Rietveld, who is linked with the industrial processes which turned workers into machine parts and have since then freed and imprisoned their descendants and ourselves.

The method of the chapter is metaphoric, even metamorphic, and its shifts are designed to destroy the idea of circumstantial connectedness. Throughout, the machine is seen as both the analogue and the antithesis of architecture, both a useful ally and a dangerous enemy.

In the Soane Museum in London hangs an astonishing painting which shows all the architect's works as models of different sizes and materials packed into a single huge room. This book aims at something similar as it packs all its diverse treasures into a single mental space. Freed from literal constraint in a phantasmagoria which is something like travel (a key experience for the most spatial of the arts, architecture), it straddles the ground between intellect and senses, realizing architecture's immediacy and its abstraction at once.

Acknowledgments

The author wishes to thank the University of North London and Helen Mallinson, Head of the School of Architecture and Interior Design, for their generous support of the writing of this book.

I do not know which to prefer,
The beauty of inflections
Or the beauty of innuendos,
The blackbird whistling
Or just after.

WALLACE STEVENS, from
"Thirteen Ways of Looking at a Blackbird"

1

Sculpture

Of all the arts sculpture is the nearest to architecture. Spatial in the most literal way, it is occasionally enterable if not habitable. Still, "sculptural" as applied to buildings has become a term of abuse, to signify a work which flaunts or ignores the whole question of use and amuses itself in indulgent explorations of form.

At its most serious, a sculptural approach to building does not rule out an interest in structure or function, but it may conceal, as it does in Gaudí, unorthodox ideas about the nature of architecture. Some of his more irresponsible "buildings" like the gateway to the Miralles estate, formerly outside and now engulfed by Barcelona, seem to delight in distortion for its own sake, twisting curved surfaces this way and that like a restless sleeper expressing the body's capacity for movement in a nearly random way.

Clearly the inspiration is organic; stone or concrete is molded like flesh, with metal members poking through which hint at a skeleton underneath, away from which the building's substance sometimes sags like a muscle losing its tension.

The first architectural principle Gaudí violates is rectangularity. Inevitably we perceive this as deviation from a norm, but for Gaudí it is reapproximation to a lost naturalness. For him the true nature of buildings is an organic sinuosity not latent in most building materials as we have come to see them.

Taking another extreme example, the nightmare world of chimneys and ventilators on the rooftop of Casa Milá, we see him inventing creatures of pronounced character to execute nondescript functions, facilitating the monotonous passage of air or smoke. If nature were to evolve these elements—a tube and a rain deflector over it—would she produce this sort of extravagance, a ribbed stalk and a knobbed helmet? The rational answer may be no; Gaudí thinks otherwise, and some idea of elaboration not strictly necessary but nonetheless determined by the circumstances in which it grew up is crucial to his ideas of nature and art. He is less whimsical than admirers like Dalí have thought, but the rules which govern his structures come from outside architecture narrowly defined.

An even more flamboyant example of a building obeying a strong nonarchitectural logic is the Einstein Tower built by Erich Mendelsohn in 1917–1921 for an institute of astrophysics. It looks as if it was molded or carved, not built. In fact the way it came about is almost the reverse of this imagined process of gradual revelation from within a single block. Mendelsohn intended a building in reinforced concrete but found that a cement shortage in postwar Germany made construction in brick more feasible. So the building has a masonry core covered in a disguise of rendering whose forms read convincingly as "deep." The whole is a fluid entity which borrows from organisms ideas like "eye" and "brow" but integrates them more fully in the general pulse than we find them in any animal except certain sea creatures.

The meaning of this integration far outstrips any such literal model. The design was informed by Mendelsohn's discussions of Einstein's physics with a friend, from which he imbibed a passionate sense of the interchangeability of matter and energy. This seemed to call the solidity, permanence, and stillness of bodies into question, with the consequence that he felt buildings should move and change, like unstable atomic particles flying through space. So the intention of these initially organic-seeming forms (more like a universal plasma than animal tissue) is different from Gaudí's. Again a seemingly whimsical form is intended as the embodiment of a particular intellectual structure, and the strongly sculptural mode is conceived as the best vehicle for this content.

Mendelsohn is sculptural at the beginning and Le Corbusier at the end of his career. In the one early hopes are dashed, while in the other early purity is muddied or enriched, depending on one's point of view. The turning point in Le Corbusier's career is widely recognized, though with hindsight premonitions of the more sculptural, less rational approach can be found in earlier stages. But when Notre-Dame du Haut at Ronchamp and the works which followed it were new they produced shock, especially among the architect's supporters.

A prominent adjunct of the new approach was a surprising, quasi-poetic appeal to organic sources for architectural ideas; thus the famous anecdote connecting the roof shape at Ronchamp with a crab shell Corb had found on a Long Island beach. He doesn't point out that he only takes a single structural principle from the model, which he inverts (was it lying upside down in the sand?). And the insistence on Long Island is simply a boast of how far sparks can jump in the genius mind.

As a painter Le Corbusier had long been interested in bodily metaphors; it is an important step to see his buildings too as part of the natural world. Thereafter it appears that architecture is not generated from architecture but from more general formal perceptions, which makes the architect's relation to reality more like the sculptor's. In the result at Ronchamp separate parts do not cohere in a bland whole. Walls and roof are discordant, walls and other walls fail to join, and at the east end the building seems to have turned itself inside out, becoming thereby a skeleton which shows inner workings on the outside, precariously. The altar and the pulpit which appear here are not the only ones in this church, but there is still the feeling that protective flesh has been peeled away leaving internal organs exposed to the elements. So again we see a building as carved, part of its substance pared away, which seems a less rational process than construction.

If in Corb and Mendelsohn there is a disturbing gap between what is meant and how it gets there, this is seen much more acutely in a work like Utzon's Sydney Opera House. Even more than Corb's it is a building which aspires to be all roof. These roofs are not content to declare themselves as roofs, but take the form of concrete shells in shapes like sprawling Gothic arches. The massed effect of eight of these placed at varying angles and elevations is that of a group of sails (the site juts into Sydney Harbour) or a number of birds in flight. In either case it is a fairly emblematic depiction, with an awkward divergence between the building and the presumed model.

Here the need to cover certain spaces is felt as a nuisance or a brake on free expression. In Corb there is no such thing as what the building would have been if it didn't need to be a building, but Utzon's would be a freestanding metal group which barely touched ground. Corb's most sculptural ideas remain indelibly architectural; Utzon seems impatient with gravity, wishing to throw it off, while the walls at Ronchamp, though restive and dynamic, are perhaps even more rooted than conventional masonry by virtue of this disquiet. The boundaries of Utzon's enclosure tend to be unhappy necessities, abrupt terminations butted against forms which abhor flat planes and true verticals when they can afford to. So the idea exists somewhere independent of and in opposition to doors and walls and the other paraphernalia of inhabiting space which have nothing to do with flight and are hard to disguise as its adjuncts.

In Gaudí strange other realities are architecturalized and become part of the act of enclosing space. But in Utzon this process is incomplete. If we come at this building from the other side and judge it against the city of which it forms part we meet a discord. The sails trying to break through are even more preposterous silhouetted against the rectangularity of nearby buildings. In these perspectives the symbolism is discontinuous with the surrounding reality and therefore makes little sense.

Of course it is possible to glory in a building's freakish separation from everything round it, like the Long Island duckling made famous by Robert Venturi, which was a roadside stand in the form of a large concrete duck seated in its own parking lot from which ducks, turkeys, chickens, and game hens were sold (moved since and turned into a souvenir stand). There is no pretense at ordaining a whole new universe: this is an acknowledged interruption like a joke in sober discourse. Though it is a distant cousin of the Einstein Tower, wearing its symbolism like a garment, it isn't entirely fair to claim the duck as a building at all. Its virtue in a serious argument is its frankness: "Let's have pretenses but parade them openly. Masks are part of reality too."

In Sydney wings and flight are connected with music, highest and most ethereal of cultural forms. On Long Island a flightless bird advertises the goods for sale inside it. In Eero Saarinen's TWA terminal, at a point on Long Island nearer to Manhattan, flying is symbolized preparatory to . . . flying. You are not entering a big bird before climbing onto the smaller one which will actually fly, but rather a sculptural emblem of the activity. Even that degree of literalness or of metaphor generates its own problems, one of which is that the building does this part of its job best before you enter it. The swoop of its eaves down to where you can almost touch them and the great continuous arc of the roof might have been visible inside too, but they aren't, because obscured by shops. In trying to house a commercial airline terminal in a romanticized dream image of the plane, Saarinen set himself an impossible task.

Even more aberrant instances exist of buildings with strong sculptural identities, like the heating plant in the Rudolf Steiner complex at Dornach in Switzerland. This takes a form somewhere between a large stalk of asparagus and a giant penis, being a tall chimney with two furnace-nodules at its base. To diversify its monotonous height it was given fleshy prongs at intervals. Perhaps it exists to fuel patients' dreams, providing them with archetypal material they must work their way out from under as part of their cure.

The building as an everyday object or dream image is taken one step further by an American hot dog stand in the shape of a hot dog, which becomes a projectile zooming through the streets by reverting to an earlier phase of its identity: it was a van before being disguised as a more or less stationary sculpture or building. Like other American products it passes off myths as childishness, but who can really tell on what journeys it takes its users? In a children's story you would climb aboard and not need to return to boring old reality for a long time.

The most powerful myths tend to be more abstract than this. The relation to ordinary reality of the Egyptian pyramids now seems problematic to say the least, and treating them as sculpture may be simply a sign of incomprehension. One can make historical excuses: they are shapes which have proved haunting to Western imaginations who knew little more than that they were tombs in the desert and thus could only view them as sculptural forms.

Apparently the Egyptian sense of the form unfolded in a direction opposite to architectural realities: the stone pyramid depicts the distribution of energy from the sun, and its slanting sides are the rays which fan out and fertilize the earth. So it is not finally a static but a dynamic, even sexual form.

Recent theories that the pyramids were left by visitors from outer space can be seen as a mechanical version of this idea; rather than inert lumps of masonry they are messengers from outside our world. It is therefore somewhat dampening to learn that the smooth-sided type evolved from a more complicated stepped ancestor, which connects it with earthbound architectural forms in which buildings have stories and heights are broken down or approached by staircases.

The pyramid as it finally evolves is a semi-abstract depiction of the most important transactions in human life, those between heaven and earth, which aligns it with many later architectural experiments where sculptural abstraction forms a way, in a perfectly usable building, of describing general features of the life lived in it, expressively enlarged.

The boldly skewed planes or platforms connected by stairs in Hans Scharoun's Haus Schminke of 1933 represent different parts or possibilities of the users' lives. This building announces vividly from afar like a pyramid seen across the desert that our moods are so different moment to moment it is as if we are constantly reoriented in relation to the ground. Although these spaces all work perfectly well, the general truth is stated so dramatically one might conclude that this building had escaped working entirely and gone over to depicting. But the striking presence of Haus Schminke is in a strange way not self-conscious, because one can feel its oddity as evolving, something which even now has not reached definitive resolution though practical thought about the building has had to stop.

If sculptural architecture means a self-regarding object in splendid isolation, Scharoun's Philharmonie in Berlin isn't it. But if it means a one-off, unique existence whose character is worked out freshly in recognition of the peculiarities of its situation. . . . The relation between parts here is informal, the result unmonumental, yet there is a sculptural vigor in the whole that architecture seldom attains. In his most radical works Scharoun moves toward an unruliness which seeks escape from all defining constraints whatever, including those of sculpture. Of course these remain suggestions never fully acted on. He never permits himself to forget the social context, so his urge to break away is always converted into new apparatus in his users' lives.

Scharoun's Philharmonie verges on sculpture in the freedom of its unforced communication, while a building like Louis Kahn's Unitarian Church in Rochester tends toward sculpture by being gnomic and not comfortably communicative. How many have recognized it easily as a church or wondered what the openings along its flanks are? Windows? doors? are they even openings, or something more fundamental still, more generalized and less useful, as if the architect is reaching back to early forms which precede anything known to us.

The keys to this design are four blank masses trapped toward the middle of the building by something like surrounding fortifications. These four towers are lighting shafts, though we would not guess it. Elements resembling archaic defenses turn up in many Kahn projects, as parking garages in plans for the center of Philadelphia or as service towers in the Richards Medical Research Building. Such "defenses" must be read nowadays for their psychological import: this is an architect who doesn't let out his meanings easily into daylight.

Lying somewhere behind Kahn's Unitarian Church in Rochester is Wright's Unity Temple in Oak Park, also built for Unitarians more than fifty years earlier. Wright's is a less monomaniacal building: he allows the two clearly separate functions— meeting hall (or church) and school—to appear as separate masses, while Kahn insists to the end (a Unitarian building must be One) on planting one inside the other. But if in some ways more compromised, Wright's design is also a mythic version of enclosure which cannot be fully rationalized. It throws out stern blank towers at the corners and makes a fair stab at windowlessness, which lets us see it as pure mass unpenetrated, with a hint of the subiime uselessness of sculpture.

A slightly later design of Wright's, the Robie House in nearby Hyde Park, is less intimidating and sinister, yet its reworking of our relation to reality is more metaphysical than functional. Strange and not entirely comfortable effects are obtained by distorting basic dimensions: space is stretched horizontally and condensed vertically, a manipulation more like a sculptor's than an architect's, which uses the building to depict a kind of landscape, identified by the literal-minded as "the prairie." Toward the end of his career in works like the Guggenheim Museum Wright became more explicit in his myth-making ambitions. Here his employment of spirals, bubbles, and other curves derived from organic models leads us back toward those sculptural buildings which imitate specific nonarchitectural realities.

Among the most elusive fashioners of sculptural identities for architecture was a sculptor himself who understood human anatomy so well it gave him a powerfully affective framework which could forego a single explicit reference. But Michelangelo turns the relation between the two inside out. Instead of an expressive clothing, the sculptural element in architecture becomes a prisoner trapped somewhere deep inside the building. In a work like the vestibule to the Laurentian Library Michelangelo creates a drama like a surgical dissection, where architectural forms are the actors in an exposure like peeling off a skin or covering, revealing columns or bones within the walls. The opposite condition is also met, blind forms suggesting secret complexity just beneath the surface. A further, more violent range of expression, as of bodies turned inside out and suffering, is suggested by the sideways volutes on the stairs.

The steps themselves are a prime example of a Mannerist conceit which occurs elsewhere too, surfaces underfoot which if not quite living tissue are alive in that they seem to be in motion. Here the steps mimic a flow of lava, and someone climbing them might easily feel that the stairs were coming down as he attempted to go up, against the current. Other Florentine steps of the period imitate soft cartilage on which the worshiper must step to approach the altar, and other works by Michelangelo practice even crueler jokes on the flesh.

Just one example from the New Sacristy at S. Lorenzo will indicate the potential for distressing sensation which this architect uncovered in the elements of the classical system. In the corners of this room the moldings are painfully close and painfully separate, a surgical rigor and discontinuity that forecasts the tormented paring away to which Michelangelo the sculptor subjected the figure of Christ both in marble and on paper in late Depositions and Crucifixions. Even earlier in his career we can grant that Michelangelo himself is the main sufferer from such rigors, as is borne out by what we know of his life. For us the agony remains mainly exhilarating because we view it as completed and organized expression.

Perhaps such reflections on distress as the subject matter of art are apropos in approaching a sort of Michelangelo of the present, Bruce Nauman. A Michelangelo in forging uncomfortable traps and cages that sit uneasily in conventional genres. Often Michelangelo's works must resign themselves to inhabiting blander preexisting buildings, and Nauman's get some of their terror from the banality of their settings. They are rooms or places imported into neutral environments, and like Michelangelo's they do the work of architecture more seriously, more probingly, than the enclosing shells whose obtuseness they must put up with.

Nauman is the sculptor as would-be architect, freed from most of the architect's responsibilities in order to make something more abstract than architecture. In his *Green Light Corridor* of 1970 Nauman squeezes a corridor effect into the back of a room when there is no evident need for the cramming. The new space is defined by the green glow from neon, a source which must be sought out. Even when the tube is located, the color remains spectral and elusive, perhaps in part because we know it arises from a current passed through a gas. Thus the space partly escapes from the place it is in.

Another Nauman installation puts one mesh cage inside another, of such dimensions that they form smaller rooms within the space we inhabit. A "door" gives admittance to the larger outer room of the two, whose volume is so nearly filled by the smaller that only the narrowest of corridors survives between them. So the viewer can inch along the perimeter in this uncomfortable space, too narrow to turn round in. Experiencing the sculpture is a kind of horrible inhabiting; one "uses" it like a building. The wire mesh which, though harsh, seemed initially a cool transparent medium begins to take on other qualities. It is an agent of humiliation, stripping away defenses.

As with Michelangelo the question arises of whether the artist is playing with the materials and hence producing willful distortions. Is the melodrama necessary? or is the viewer turned into a prisoner on a whim? Few can wholeheartedly like what Nauman is saying, but many will acknowledge that he gives an impressive density of organization to his ideas, and that his traps are so ingeniously constructed that they teach us something about rooms in general.

Another contemporary sculptor who produces more strictly architectural effects, Richard Serra, has brought the idea of the corridor, one of Nauman's main stocks in trade, to one of the most shapeless public spaces in Europe, the Place de la Concorde in Paris. This space converges on a vista which now (with the arch/office building at La Défense) terminates several miles away. Instead of trying to match this scale, Serra's *Clara Clara* creates a competing spatial experience with two curved walls like hedges which start farther apart, converge to a narrow opening, then end farther apart again. The net effect is to materialize a corridor for an instant, then let it fade away. A drawing for this project reveals his powerful interest in spatial tolerances: he alerts us to how much of architectural experience is about nearness without touching or convergences which don't become explicit.

In his work for the City of London called *Fulcrum* Serra sets himself more directly in competition with architecture. This consists of four tall steel plates which act like walls, leaning toward and away from each other. It outdoes the surrounding structures, being both more monolithic and more sensuous than they. Its textures are more immediate, its putting together is clearer, and most of all it concerns itself with bigger spatial ideas—convergence and divergence, or coming into being and receding from being. *Fulcrum* is the philosophy of constructed spaces as against its neighbors' practice; sculpture is the place where architecture freed from various duties finds room to understand itself.

There are other recent sculptors whose work, though less centrally architectural, illuminates some of the preoccupations of architects. Joseph Beuys often focuses on degenerative or culminative process, like the congealing and slow rotting of animal fat—an accelerated version of weathering in buildings—welcoming which is a sign of not wanting to hide from the truth and so facing up to what we and the world are made of.

Andy Goldsworthy's work focuses on such change to the point of impossibility, stringing together dead leaves and frail twigs in spirals derived from sea shells or in cones which look like medieval footwear. It is so quintessentially flimsy that it is more like an anti-architecture, if one can admit any relation at all. *Snowballs in April* must be one of the worst offenders. Large snowballs laced with mud and straw (which would accelerate melting) were constructed in February, then carted to a food storage plant to be brought out in April and displayed in two orderly rows down the aisles of an empty industrial building in Glasgow. It took a few weeks for them to melt, and that was the duration of the work. At first glance their geometry is utterly at odds with the angular surroundings and their precariousness makes them absurd. But of course the ability to last is a pressing issue for any work of art and in a special form for architecture—will it stay up and will it stay useful? Goldsworthy depicts a world which won't hold still, where form-giving is accepted as a slippery slope which one keeps sliding to the bottom of.

Many of his works show a kinship with the eighteenth-century genre of sham ruins. To call Goldsworthy's effects or Soane's collages in his own house in Lincoln's Inn Fields "sham" is misleading, of course. Both of them create art of unlikely materials and are obsessed with decay. Soane makes architecture out of sculptural detritus, and the result is an unplaceable hybrid. In the Dome at the center of his house there are not "walls" anymore but an intermittently visible framework encrusted with fragments like an obscene natural growth. It is one of the most intentionally bewildering spaces in the world. Was it originally more solid, or simpler and less variegated? Is it growing or decaying? At what point in its life have we come? Soane's den is a kind of antithesis to Pope's grotto (which made sculpture out of curious natural fragments— glittering minerals and gnarled shells). Soane naturalizes architecture by situating it in the unconscious, a realm which is naturally obscure.

Soane makes uninhabitable rooms which become more interesting with every hole time pokes in them, so the imaginary narrative runs. In Aldo Rossi's drawings his architectural proposals often look like a serious kind of bric-a-brac. Buildings share a table top with a Coke can and pack of cigarettes of almost architectural size. This way of presenting the ideas encourages one to see them as objects which have their real existence in the mind and the city as a conception slightly abstract, independent like a sculpture or a ruin.

Rossi's most engrossing project, the cemetery at Modena, allows him to experiment with such forms largely emptied of content and life. Of all these the Columbarium is most striking, a house as a roofless sleeve full of "windows" whose ambiguous or negative character is visible a long way off. One could perversely describe sculpture as emptied architecture, whose forms are not expected to do anything, only to be. But Rossi goes further than the sculptor who removes the human figure from combat so it may be contemplated. His volumes feel like ones which have had something taken away, places in which something is missing. It is hard to say why this impression is so strong. He is happier doing tombs, as some neoclassical sculptors were doing corpses, and one can only speculate that contrary to his conscious theories Rossi finds architecture realer when the armature is isolated and the life sucked out of it, for then the underlying archetype speaks without interference.

In the so-called *Scientific Autobiography* (which is a stream of poetic images in unrigorous dreamlike sequence) Rossi tells a revealing story of how he climbed a hollow metal statue as a child and looked out over his native town. He picks out this experience, repeated a few times, as critical in pointing him toward architecture. The figure was a local saint with his hand raised in blessing over the town. But as far as Rossi can tell the spiritual pretensions of the colossus leave him unmoved. In fact the unfeeling mineral chill of the material excites the child with an idea of artifice existing in pure detachment from feeling. So later his Types can be rather brutally expressed without concessions to friendly textures or proportions. This large enterable sculpture gave him the idea of buildings which it's a surprise to find are enterable, whose intention is only incidentally to provide a comfortable home for the body but which exist rather to suggest to the mind those abstract and enduring models which say simply house, school, tower, rotunda, chimney. This urge to find what never varies or varies inessentially means that, unlike most architects, Rossi goes on rehearsing his designs after they are built, and that their most satisfying forms are graphic reworkings like wooden toys demonstrating the possibility of combining a roof and a bridge and situating them among towers to make a city.

Nothing could be further from this conception than sculpture as an embellishment of architecture. One can almost say that the idea of detail itself is anathema to Rossi, for it opens the door to a long process of qualifying and obscuring the main idea. In this he resembles the radical architects of the French Enlightenment whose bizarre heir he is. Once you open the gate, where do you stop? The result is inevitably less single and pure, a hybrid in an absolutely unacceptable sense. Rossi's work is ambiguously situated between human use (architecture) and pure form (sculpture), between something which is really a house and something which discusses "house."

But a building like the Doge's Palace in Venice is hybrid in a more insidious way. As one turns its corner (to which one is brought by a bridge like a scaffold which crosses a small canal) one is arrested by a scene at eye level. This is carved in deep relief and spills over the borders which the architecture tries to maintain. The subject is Noah drunk; he sprawls beside a tree whose trunk twists past his leg and whose branches shade him. He should be lying down but the space available won't allow it; for he is part of an architectural element, the corner post of an arcade, and if he were laid out flat he would obscure the structural logic even more.

Ruskin was detained by this figure for a year or more. In the end he extracted from it the whole history of the Middle Ages in Venice. To him it seemed natural that such meanings should get stuck on buildings and distract the viewer. Interest and significance weren't distributed evenly through the fabric of a building, or indivisible, or always separable from literary narrative. Ruskin's digressive treatments of sculpture on the face of the Doge's Palace are a powerful argument for architectural hybrids and for an impure, hybrid approach to them.

Around the turn of the century on the fringes of Europe a certain kind of sculptural decoration became a badge of nationhood and embodied a particular romantic conception of the psyche. In places like Finland and Hungary buildings sprouted figures from local myths and legends together with strictly local species of plants and animals. These eruptions are later phases of the same movement which prompted James Macpherson to produce partly fictitious reconstructions of ancient Gaelic poetry.

It wasn't feasible to house banks in primitive huts, but architects like Armas Lundgren and Lars Sonck produced designs whose decoration summoned up vanished ancestral spirits and gave their young and intending country a decidedly murky history. It was inarticulate, but that made it unanswerable. Who could argue with wood demons and damsels who lived at the bottom of lakes? No medieval cathedral ever carried a more insistent moral and political message than these twentieth-century designs which used sculptural ornament to derationalize architecture.

However outlandish these Western versions of the fusion of architecture and sculpture, by comparison with Hindu temples they seem halfhearted. In buildings like the Rajarani temple at Bhuvaneswar structure and decoration become one, and the form of the whole obeys a logic dictated in part by the stories it carries. Churning figures give way to vigorous corrugations at which one needs to look hard to make sure that they aren't figural. The activities portrayed by hundreds of tiny figures are generally indecorous, even abandoned, by our standards. For all its symmetrical regularity of form, to Western eyes such a building flirts with the blurring of all distinctions and the end of meaningful sequence.

A homemade version of an Indian temple complex took a French rural postman thirty-three years to build at Hauterives near Lyons. He had gone to Algeria on military service and was an avid reader of popular magazines and encyclopedias. From such sources he got his ideas about the variety and unity of all history and culture. The whole concoction is deeply and continuously exotic and jumbles together mythical beings and historical personages through his misremembering of his sources. It bristles with figures in a masonry which resembles coral reefs not only in its corrugated texture but in its accretive growth. This phantasm sits next door to the postman's house, but he christened it *Palais idéal* to express its elevation above and removal from everyday life, so he is under no illusion that one could actually live in his construction: it provides the setting for sleepwalking dreams, with its larger-than-life population which recapitulates the history and geography of the world.

Perhaps the Facteur Cheval's palace of the ideal is the ultimate tendentious work, but the sermon has been hopelessly compromised by amplification and revision. He never achieves the vulgar clarity of statement which one ordinarily finds in bombastic works like the Soviet Pavilion at the 1937 Paris Exhibition, or its unbuilt fulfillment, the Palace of the Soviets intended for Moscow, a design evolved over a long period until it was much too ambitious for Soviet technical capacities and was allowed to slip out of sight. But if all the various proposals for this ceremonial monument, or even a few of Stalin's favorites among those submitted, had been built at a tenth their proper size, a kind of *Palais idéal* might have resulted.

The trouble with the winning design was that it was both a composite and a monolith at the same time. To get the maximum power from its two components, sculpture and architecture, they were placed on top of each other, the world's tallest statue on the world's biggest tower, a crude idea of how complex wholes are formed, worthy of the builders of Babel. Ideological clarity is here defeated by aesthetic confusion. And in any case ancient Egyptian sculptors had really said the last word on gargantuan figures at

Abu Simbel several millennia earlier. There they had had the mind-numbing idea of repeating the same enormous image of Rameses II four times, seated, like a building.

The impulse to anchor buildings even more firmly by attaching sculpture to them is of course diametrically opposed to the attitudes which gained ascendancy in the Baroque. At that moment, in Rome, architecture seems continually on the point of turning into sculpture. Bernini's colonnade which extends the forecourt of St. Peter's into an ellipse shows a huge classical order losing its fixity and springing into movement like a whole series of athletic figures. Inside the basilica Bernini's improvements include the baldacchino in bronze and gilt, a miniature building like a transitory awning, or a bit of architectural energy which has torn itself loose from the walls in order to act more freely in space.

This general principle received the most ingenious elaboration in Bavarian Rococo. At Ottobeuren the pulpit is a little room which grows away from the wall, whose elements threaten to liquefy and lose their shape completely. At times the architectural frame seems to exist primarily for a lot of plaster babies to climb on, who are made of plaster burnished to something between porcelain and marble. These children must have a dim memory of classical system because they tumble at just the intervals where a series of missing pilasters would fall. But they are also busy shredding any sense we have of stable substance. In their hands the "walls" of the little structure are converted to stretched, looped, and cascading cloth which trails off at the edges in tassels like water droplets.

Remembering that this was once a simpler architectural entity may seem like Protestant accountancy, but really the movement is fully delightful only when understood as deviation from a set of outworn rules. Rococo makes one think that sculptural impulses in architecture are overlaid on or burst out from a prior, more stolid phase. Columns find their way to figures only quite late, whatever Vitruvius may say.

Rococo grace often covers the most flagrant violation of architectural decorum, but never really approaches certain recent efforts. A kind of extreme is reached with the Coop Himmelblau factory in Austria where, in an ostensibly industrial building, a sculptural drama is contrived from baldly displayed structure. Perhaps the effect is just as illusory in its own way as Rococo confections of paint and plaster. But like them it is persuasive, and what one thinks one has seen is the ultimate colonization of the realm of function by the sculptor's insistence on play as the governing mode.

2
Machines

The idea of the machine has been one of the inspirations of modern architecture, much more powerful than sculpture as a sometimes stern, sometimes liberating notion of what buildings could be. This exceedingly influential conception still comes loaded with partisan feeling.

Machines are many things—linked sequences of moving parts which perform work, externalizations of human action in stylized form, resulting in alien sorts of existence which move in nonorganic ways; concentrations of ingenuity, device piled on device, until they defeat easy comprehension; and of course an escape from feeling into an objective realm. It is hard if not impossible to separate the dreams we have about them from the useful functions they perform. Increasingly people have wondered how adequate it ever is to describe machines in terms of rationally plotted uses. Isn't there always a metaphysical or fantastic component and hasn't this become ever clearer as they proliferate, until they absorb much of our time and thought?

There is a missing piece of the puzzle which may help illuminate how we have come to attribute such significance to the machine and at the same time liberate us from restrictive views of its potential. This is the Renaissance notion of the machine as a device refined and aristocratic, not grubby and instrumental, the machine as a kind of entertainment.

In this category ingenuity and usefulness are not necessarily in strict harmony. Even in a sixteenth-century design for a mechanical aqueduct to serve Toledo, complexity appears to be sought for its own sake. Instead of a continuous trough, this device consists of a whole series of dipping arms which break the flow into segments and produce a more complicated movement than the flow of water they take the place of. It is utopian, not in its goal but in its elaboration of a simple task: the sort of dense mechanism appropriate to the inside of a clock has been extended over an entire landscape.

A more typical example of this kind of machine would be one of those table centerpieces which revolved and sprayed perfumed water, moving in dancelike but mechanical ways. Dance or similar ritualized movement is in fact the pattern for the operation of these machines, which like processions in the street or ceremonial combats in urban squares exist to connect cultural to cosmic order. Human mechanisms take their cue from the most embracing and satisfying coherence in the world, the coordination of the stars and planets in their spheres.

In such pageantry an allegorical conceit often went hand in hand with mechanical intricacy. A theater stage was perhaps the most highly elaborated venue of all, where the concentration of devices was matched by their extremely ephemeral nature: a vast preparation leading to a transient result. It seems to have been a point of pride that the intricate machines and costumes for a Jacobean court masque should be used only once and then destroyed. The acme of this approach is a fireworks display, which in the early seventeenth century still retained its connection to the battlefield. The extravagance of fireworks would remind one of a far more wasteful outburst, irrevocable in a different way. Some of the earliest laments at excessive mechanization are disillusioned commentaries on the moral influence of mechanically operated long-range weapons which gunpowder made possible.

Fireworks are examples of machines as squanderers not economizers of energy, reveling in expenditure and the exercise of power. Elizabethan prodigy houses sometimes look ephemeral too, though we know they are not, like table ornaments blown up to unheard-of size. They are unequaled in other countries for outrageous display, though not grander in scale than comparable buildings in France and Italy.

Wollaton Hall near Nottingham, one of the crudest and liveliest of all prodigy houses, like a stage set and a piece of serious fortification at once, was financed by an early industrial fortune made in mining local coal. Coming on its startling silhouette for the first time, one might fantasize that an old fortified core has been trapped in a later ruff of frilly towers which terminate in chimneys disguised as classical columns and balustrades dotted with figures.

The five towerlike projections form a set of independent buildings when seen from the roof, which functions also, in standard Elizabethan fashion, as a viewing platform. The roof belongs to another world from which everything looks different, and the scale of the parts which jut above it is entirely transformed when we view them from this artificial ground plane.

Wollaton is like a machine in number and diversity of parts. These do not move, it is true, but they look as if they could creak into life, an illusion bred in part by the nonmatching character of the bits. Everything is stone, even the iron rings carved on pedestals at ground level, the curled-up leather ornament under many windows, the jewels and cannon balls embedded across the facade. Perhaps these oddities show that a Netherlandish pattern book was the source. On the printed page a range of substances were represented in the same graphic medium, but were meant to be translated into polished marble, bronze, or wood. The misunderstandings in the English derivative, where everything is interpreted in stone, like a kit assembled in the wrong order, convey a perverse energy. Moving further and further from its structural origins, classical detail becomes expressive gadgetry, like an overcrowded Japanese instrument panel.

The culmination of Elizabethan love of artifice and its objectification in gadgetry came in the adornment of the human body. The process continued until the body disappeared under a disfiguring load of gems and other hard substances laid out in rigid and unyielding patterns. The most fantastical versions of all were the portraits, so called, of Queen Elizabeth.

If portraits are personal and individual then these are not portraits, which show a woman made into an artifact, a huge bit of jewelry organized according to a different logic than the body's. She has been made over as if for certain uses, but what are they? Does this machine work? Undoubtedly it does; the human being is alienated into a powerful arrangement of stiff leaves in gold thread each in its little compound, proclaiming the queen as the controller of natural process, as a great metaphor, and that which holds together all the diversity of the world.

Elizabeth's clothing obliterates the body underneath, in favor of idealized but mechanical suggestions of power. Asked to design a machine, Michelangelo reintroduces the body unexpectedly in the alien context. His proposals for the fortification of Florence threatened by German mercenaries are among his most interesting projections. He concentrates on corners and gates, simple features which take on a daunting complexity as he attempts to make every possible angle of attack correspond to a line of fire from within.

Much abstracting and sublimating intelligence is focused on the crude matter of defense. Under pressure of necessity he synthesizes crystalline and skeletal organization, making buffers and shields which resemble ball and socket joints or entrance filters with the unfolding symmetry of Rohrschachs.

Most of the extant drawings show these conceptions in plan only, and it is hard to judge how much of the flavor of standard Mannerist ornament, greatly enlarged, would have come through in the swathed external elevations. The plan is an X ray which gives insight into workings which would finally be hidden, like a sculpture inside a packing case.

These gadgetlike proposals put one on the lookout for similar transmutations of human form in Michelangelo's peacetime architecture. They reveal attitudes to scale which are indeed reflected in the library and funerary chapel at S. Lorenzo, where elements of human anatomy regularly appear at many times life size. In Elizabeth's portraits the human body is deliberately alienated from organic form; in Michelangelo's defenses, mechanisms are given flexible bodies, a humanizing which might have seemed just a grisly joke if they had ever made it off the drawing board.

A different kind of necessity drove young artists during the Russian Revolution to learn from and emulate machines. They weren't designing for war but in a war-torn environment, which decreed that art mustn't look like art anymore. In that particular ambience painters became sculptors and sculptors became engineers—everyone felt a strong pull toward more practical or at least practical-seeming ends.

In revealing photos taken in 1921 at the second Obmokhu (shorthand for Society of Young Artists) exhibition we get a strong sense of the exciting disruption these young artists hoped to cause, but also of the boundaries they continued to recognize. Conventional gallery spaces are shown loosely packed with explosive devices. These are freestanding but flimsy constructions consisting of sticks and wires, many of which lurch sideways, thrusting out arms containing wheels suggesting motion. A powerful centrifugal force has torn these devices loose from the walls and from the pedestals on which art usually offers itself to the contemplator. An energy too excitable to be easily harnessed is unleashed, and yet important proprieties are observed: these art workers still choose to show their work in a museum. Categories are breaking down but the realm of art survives intact, and art ceases to be instantly recognizable only in order to make its presence more aggressively felt.

The most famous example from this time of art as a machine of architectural scale is Vladimir Tatlin's proposed monument to the Third International. It resembles the objects in the Obmokhu photos, a teetering and defiantly unbeautiful structure without any kind of smooth wrapping. The key difference is that Tatlin's tower would have risen many hundreds of feet into the air, its overweening size showing that the sculptor has been deceived by the inflated rhetoric of the revolution. Words are cheap and symbols are too: the greatest political movement of the modern world needs the tallest commemoration. But this grandiosity has doomed it to remain a concept or rather an ornament, like a Renaissance centerpiece, to be carried through the streets of Moscow as a thirteen-foot model which takes four bearers to lift.

Part of its appeal and its absurdity is how much meaning it aspires to encapsulate. Eiffel's tower had few such pretensions and remains a relatively straightforward engineering feat. Tatlin's, contrarily, looks inefficient and overbuilt but holds a wealth of symbolism within its heavy web.

Tatlin's frame is more massive partly because it contains elaborate accommodation. There are four rotating solids, each traveling at a different speed to remind us of the hour, the day, the month, and the year, each a geometrical archetype (hemisphere, cylinder, cone, and cube), and each housing a particular function (information, administration, recreation, and conferences). So the memorial turns out to be an explanatory model of the cosmos bringing enlightenment to a backward population in spectacular form. Except that it remains an imaginary mechanism, like an alchemical transformation. The symbolism is resolved; the mode of support and means of rotation have not been worked out. Tatlin's tower remains that paradoxical quantity, the utopian machine.

Other products of the same years repeat these mistakes or ambitions. Ladovsky's proposal for a block of flats like a giant crane has again resolved everything at the level of symbolism. Like Tatlin's tower this dwelling is a vector or beacon pointing toward a new future, but Ladovsky's "practicality" is if anything more unlikely than Tatlin's: here symbolism has triumphed over the most elementary structural principles.

Floor plans accompanying the perspective view of this project reveal further violations of prerevolutionary pieties, especially that of right angles in internal spaces. The proposed division into flats looks like the pattern when glass shatters or the segments on an insect's stomach. Instead of boring boxes the new life will provide interesting splinters and slivers of space which encourage restless activity. A jerky movement learned from machines now appears in human thought and behavior.

Before the Vesnin brothers got a chance to build anything outdoors, Alexander Vesnin had produced stage sets which are exceedingly architectural but, unlike their Renaissance predecessors, do not imitate buildings which actually exist in the world outside. Instead they present a kind of essence not unlike a piece of Renaissance strapwork come alive. The Vesnin set for *The Man Who Was Thursday* of 1922, with its transparent towers and connecting gangways, is a pure transmission system in which actors become the cogs or pivots. Architectural projects by the Vesnins from the same period are similarly lucid and undisguised, like the winning competition entry of 1922–1923 for a Palace of Culture in Moscow.

This is one of the most perfect renditions of a building as a working mechanism, in which a tall rectangular solid is tied to a low elliptical one by means of a hefty bridge. Above these volumes a web of wires and masts bristles, suggesting radio transmissions which hold the whole structure within their force field. They intimate an ideal version of the building as a set of messages in constant flux.

But different renderings of the project give utterly different impressions of what kind of machine it is. The refined perspective in spidery line described above makes it a net of tentative impulses, almost an electrical phenomenon and nothing more. Other gloomy, shaded views make it an outmoded but reliable workhorse which forecasts the five-year plans of the Stalin era. Depending on one's vision of society one could have it either way: meeting halls, bureaus, and theaters, so restlessly separated and combined in this proposal and served by preposterous numbers of stairs (to express constant social movement), lend themselves to the idea of society as the liberator of every divergent impulse or as the final defeat of individuation and private desire.

As is well known, Russia in the 1930s experienced a forced reversion to classical prototypes, perverted toward gargantuan forms that signify the power of the state rather than an atomized proletariat. While this was taking place in reality, on the plane of fantasy Jakob Chernikov pursued the vision of the machine as the liberator of both architecture and humanity at once.

In 1933 he published a hundred designs for impossibly lavish factories, refineries and power stations which continue to exercise a powerful fascination because they are so entirely uncompromising. They posit an ideal world of limitless resources or insatiable requirements where processing plants stretch on as far as the eye can see, made up of interesting forms which repeat themselves in generous series. There are wide spaces and clear links between the dispersed parts, but there is never any smoke, nor a single workman nor messy piles of the product nor waste from the process nor signs of transport to and from this self-contained world.

Colors are magical—metallic blues, reds, oranges, and blacks. In this place energy never grows tired or old, nothing breaks, night and winter are unknown. I am told Chernikov's structures are sound and ingeniously engineered, not the irresponsible affairs they seem to me (cantilevers on spidery V-props); nonetheless his designs look more purely theatrical than the Vesnin stage sets. They are not incidents but worlds, and they sit in an ideal space which stretches to infinity. Earlier, in the mid-1920s, he had produced more serious if less overtly practical designs. This series shows pieces of machinery enlarged to building size. These are powerful because their impossibility is kept insistently before us: we can see that these machines-as-buildings are not enterable, while at the same time no one is big enough to operate them.

The contemporary Japanese architect Shin Takamatsu also makes mechanical forms mythical by enlargement. Some of his buildings of the early 1980s look like devices with many moving parts, often threatening—blades and rotary disks recur, suggesting slicing and cutting. These intimations of grandiose and dangerous function are completely dispelled by interior spaces which owe much to 1930s kitsch. His recent work is more stolid externally than those classic instances of flamboyant gadgetry from the 1980s, the Week Building, The Ark, and Origin 3. By the time we reach the Kirin complex designed in 1991–1992 Takamatsu's work has become monumental and undynamic. But for a brief period he produced buildings like no others, quintessential expressions from the heartland of technology run riot (Japan), menacing idols which are one of the most extreme fulfillments of placing one's faith in machines.

Against this idea of the machine as a terrifying being should be set the machine as pure rational system, which employs the minimum of material to cover the maximum area without an imposing effect. The seminal ancestor of this form of the building-as-machine is the Crystal Palace, thrown up quickly in Hyde Park to house the Great Exhibition of 1851. It derives from garden greenhouses, lightest and most elementary enclosures, representing a return to first principles in the interest of unobtrusive economy. Such buildings (barely acknowledged to merit the name of building by some) start from the question: what can a building do without? Walls, pretty nearly, is the answer: they have become flimsy membranes held in place by the least forceful of frames, elements which seem to leave no room for creating an architectural impression as conventionally understood.

The Crystal Palace no longer looks radical, but inheritors of its hardheaded nonmonumental ethos like Cedric Price preserve something of the original freshness which irritated Ruskin. Like Paxton's, Price's ideas reach a preliminary fulfillment when scrawled on a napkin. When built or partially built (more about the appeal of that option in a minute), they lose some of the clarity of their diagram form.

A work like the Interaction Centre in Kentish Town seems to admit more affinity with construction photos than with images of finished buildings. It is based on a grid some of whose divisions haven't yet been filled in. Incomplete roofing-in of the steel frame leaves openings for life to develop and lets the architect suggest an unpredictable future. The building reveals itself best from above (a railway viaduct passes fortuitously near) and appears to be bursting its bounds; any envelope at all is seen to be accidental. Thus the design remains an idea, or a net in which various bits have got lodged like bugs in the radiator grille of a car. Like these insects, the gelled or completed elements of the structure are significant as clues to a process, signs of activity which buildings can't entirely contain. So this work is like a machine not in its strict logic but in its absence of extraneous baggage and its unprogrammatic linkages.

Sometime in the eighteenth century Jacques de Vaucanson, the French builder of automata, constructed a duck with over a thousand moving parts which allowed it to eat, digest, and excrete its food as its natural model would have done. This mechanical duck isn't made of skin, muscles, and feathers but of geared linkages which its exterior does not allow us to predict and which don't "go with" the idea of a duck.

Looking at a building by Cedric Price is like seeing inside the duck: we are not used to this clear a view of how not just our equipment but our lives are supposed to work. But naked analysis of function has an alienating effect, cutting us off from everyday life. Unlike the duck's digestion, the diagrams of activity found in the Interaction Centre are patterns the users wear out and want to revise, at which point they find that even a building this flexible is holding them to rules they don't wish to keep, so they erect Portacabins under the steel frame which was meant for easy roofing over when more space was required. There are precedents in the world of machines for devices with functioning and obsolete parts side by side. Interaction may be on the way to joining ruined abbeys imperfectly converted into country houses.

Even Palladian country houses have their Price-like moments, staircases which are foci of mechanical ingenuity more or less undisguised. In early modernist experiments in Germany a glazed stairwell became a metaphor for the aggressive dynamism of modem architecture, and vertical movement had powerful ideological overtones.

Long before, Palladio and his imitators had exploited the potential of stairs as bald depictions of complicated transfers. At Chiswick House the entrance stair, outside but attached to the building, is almost the tail which wags the dog, more emblematic than narrowly functional, organizing the visitor into a strange regularity of movement.

Mies van der Rohe made a floating staircase in painted steel a feature of the main room rather than something to be concealed in a corridor when he reconstructed the Arts Club in Chicago. For all its elegance this device also makes prescriptions about behavior, an occasion for rule-giving firmly grasped by this architect.

One of Piranesi's *Carceri* shows a fantastic multiplication of the staircase where too many connections produce a maze. Never has a building been so full; masonry modeled on ancient Roman brick-work but now executed in stone becomes a means of clogging rather than creating space.

Although it is not a prison or terrifying, the Centre Pompidou in Paris provokes comparison with Piranesi rather than Mies. It conjures up a vision of rationality as confusing, and if its escala-tors don't eat up the space, they provide much of the visual ex-citement on the facade and effectively obscure the monotony which lies behind. It is one apotheosis of the stair, mechanized, with its own power of movement, but like Piranesi's it prompts a feeling that all such journeys within buildings are somewhat gratuitous. The purpose of one system is (or purports to be) bondage, of the other, play; they are not so far apart.

The tradition of the building as a machine traced here from the Crystal Palace to the Centre Pompidou has a surprising mentor, a structural rationalist who spent much of his working life study-ing and repairing Gothic buildings. Some of Viollet-le-Duc's most up-to-date experiments remained theoretical, like the hybrid vaulting systems in iron and stone illustrated in the *Entretiens*. His essential contribution to modern architecture was to rescue ratio-nality from classicism via a startling new view of the significance of Gothic.

Gothic as seen by Viollet is rational not spiritual, a kind of problem-solving which pays scant heed to decorum and arrives at its oddities of structure and proportion while seeking answers to physical questions about weight, lighting, and various economies of construction. Thanks to Viollet we are able to see the great French cathedrals as feats of engineering to which no medieval mists cling.

All cathedrals are machines, and Beauvais is the starkest in-stance of all because only a truncated fragment and, since it is the crossing and chancel which survive, a concentrate of maximum structural daring. From afar it is easier to gauge how much of the weight and supporting structure have been thrown outside the walls in a system of buttresses like the building's skeleton or a lightweight scaffold. Many apparently decorative features—attenuated pinnacles and vertical paneling on the infrequent expanses of unbroken masonry—are enhancements not disguises of the main structural idea, a forest of vertical members held together by relatively light webbing. Inside, obsessive concentration on a specialized goal is even more apparent. The space culminates entirely out of our reach, a kind of single-minded pursuit which is one definition of rationality.

A surprising kinship with Gothic appears in a contemporary exponent of expressive structure. As in Gothic, there are paradoxes over the relation between the machinelike and the organic in the work of Santiago Calatrava, who has made his name with mechanisms like bridges and stations where structural ideas predominate. At the Stadelhofen railway station in Zurich we find the Gothic delight in repetitive expression of structural members, particularly in joints which suggest movement. On the upper level the skeletal canopy is pure rib without any infill, like the diagram of a vault. On the level where trains pass and stop, canopies which curve with the track are held up by sloping supports which echo the steep terrain where city walls used to be and also mimic the movement of the trains, seeming to flex in anticipation of the rumbling invasion.

Tedious necessities like pedestrian walkways over the tracks provoke outbursts of ingenuity. One of these bridges comes very near to a version of Viollet's stone and iron vaults: Calatrava's favorite materials steel and concrete form a similar hybrid with a powerful message; they are bone and flesh and a sign of a deep metaphoric stratum in this work. The materials are those of machines, but the underlying forms of organization are organic: an animal skeleton with its trunk and limbs, legs and wings. The disguise via technology isn't truly a disguise: buildings can't really be creatures so Calatrava's borrowing is limited to principles of structure and general proportions of hard to soft matter. Isolated elements may have a specific organic source, but architectural wholes, at least in his strongest projects, will not resemble single organisms. Animals have two or four legs; buildings have dozens, which is one good reason for playing down whatever bizarre individuality one might be tempted to give them.

Some of Calatrava's most interesting work has taken the form of prosthetic appliances attached to or inserted in other designers' buildings, like his series of roofs for a school in Wohlen. To add roofs to someone else's building is either an extremely ungrateful task or the chance to concentrate on structure with an intensity which would be out of place if one had responsibility for the whole.

At Wohlen the entrance canopy is an independent device, like a laboratory demonstration of certain bending and twisting opportunities. The result is strongly skewed according to a simple logic—as one half of the V-shape grows, the other shrinks. The result is a crest or wing which flares and subsides, sweeping away from and returning to the ground.

Perhaps his greatest predecessor in the attempt to derive the forms of machines from those of organisms is Leonardo da Vinci, an experimental scientist, inventor of mechanisms, and dedicated observer of a vast range of life and movement. Leonardo's bridges look like skeletons and his plant drawings sometimes resemble mechanisms. One in particular, showing the whorl of leaves of a star-of-Bethlehem with flower stalks rising above them, is an astonishing instance of uncovering a single ruling principle without losing the ripple of peculiar life.

To pursue the relation between particular and general in this drawing, we need to range alongside it others in which Leonardo uncovers the same form in vastly different contexts. At least two present themselves: a sheet with an old man seated next to ripple patterns produced artificially in a fast-moving stream, and one of the Deluge drawings which shows a whole city and a great mountain range caught in a swirling cataclysm of water, wind, and dust.

There's an energy in the star-of-Bethlehem's growth that threatens to break loose into literal motion. The fall of the old man's beard is a weaker version of the stream's turbulence, generated like the springing of leaves from a single center but moving in a single direction instead of spreading out equally in circular ripples. The catastrophic storm shows similar forces raised to a much higher power. After seeing pictures of destruction like the Deluge one can detect in Leonardo's most placid images signs that this great analytic power tends to destructuring. So the consonance between the beard and the stream isn't so much a peaceful metaphor as it is an X ray of hostile forces.

Leonardo's dissections, of bodily systems or mechanical workings, have never been improved on. His pictures of genito-urinary function or of a screw device for field irrigation are both clearer and fuller than anyone else's. Yet they provoke a deep unease. His procedure depends on the uninhibited use of the mind as a tool. Most modern observers praise this as a truly scientific approach. No one can deny the power of his analysis, but some will object to its heartlessness. An amoral curiosity rules—most vividly in the images of destruction, but also if more discreetly in the nonmilitary mechanisms. Leonardo depicts horrors without feeling them and moves toward the objectified consciousness all too familiar since, but new when it surfaces in his perception of the world as a series of mechanisms to be understood by taking them apart.

There is a Renaissance institution which corresponds very nearly to Leonardo's brilliant dissections of natural systems and his parallel reconstructions of them as mechanical process. It is the museum, which is better seen as the aftermath of dissection than as the primary analytic act. A museum occurs in a world which has come apart and which someone feels the need of putting back together. In the last two centuries the territory of the museum has been radically extended until anything which can be named or thought can become its organizing principle. An eighteenth-century drawing shows a large room lined floor to ceiling with a nonrepeating collection of delicate machines. It is fascinating to see scientific instruments themselves, agents of atomization, become the objects of the collector's scrutiny, who thereby aims to form a disjointed picture of the whole range of human inquiry. The devices in such a collection, many of them lodged on unreachably high shelves, no longer participate in actual measurement and experiment—no single scientist could devise uses for all of them—but they give the observer an almost instantaneous grasp of one discipline or fragment of learning after another. He is simultaneously aware of the diversity of human speculation and its unencompassability, another name for its incoherence.

For us pictures of seventeenth-century picture galleries possess great charm, because they show how imperfectly the idea of the museum was developed in that unsophisticated time. Paintings are crowded like tiles on the walls with only the grouting of their frames between. Many are far above eye level; the lowest almost touch the floor. Sometimes insects on pins in a glass case are arranged symmetrically, big ones at the bottom, small at the top, two blue ones across from each other, the eyes in a facelike pattern. So with these paintings—portraits match portraits and landscapes are mirrored by others. Never mind if the times and places are different. Any single element is a piece in the puzzle, a part which has its function in the mechanism. The meaning of individual bits is devalued—these painters would have produced something entirely different if given their slots in this jigsaw and told to fill them. The whole is difficult to comprehend, yet it would not be fair to call it frivolous. Real mental strain, not idle pattern-making, has generated these strange conglomerates, which are proto-scientific in their attitude to painting. In most of our museums the transformation has gone much further and individual paintings take their places in a large apparatus called history.

In architecture such a radically dissected world makes one of its most attractive appearances in the work of Gerrit Rietveld. Space is discontinuous in the Schröder house in Utrecht, having come apart into thin flakes, rectangular solids, and bodiless lines. The geometric consistency of the sources does not prepare one for the disjunctive overall effect which Rietveld contrives from them. Even single objects collapse into or articulate themselves as myriad pieces. This is not so surprising when they are radio sets encased in glass to reveal their workings, but reaches unexpected heights in the famous stick-chairs which call into question all the conventional means for erecting a chair above the ground.

This is an idea he kept returning to: in a child's high chair and numerous grown-up versions. Sometimes, as in the most famous design in primary colors, it becomes more painterly and one of the nearest approaches furniture has ever made to purely graphic effect. But the essential idea remains the same throughout: the world reseen as a succession of distinct acts. So the leg meeting the seat isn't two but four entities negotiating a settlement. Sometimes it works like simple double vision: you didn't think there were, and in some sense there aren't, so many separate elements to reality.

But however much like pleasant toys Rietveld's equipment for living seems, underlying it is a sense that nothing is safe or certain. After modern physics and modern art one can't take even chairs for granted. They are as arbitrary and coercive as other machines, like the Jacquard looms that Rietveld's chairs so uncannily resemble, which trap skilled workers in a narrow range of movement for a whole lifetime of labor. Modern architecture's love affair with machines often stems from and ends in a sense of drastically circumscribed possibility.

3

The **Body**

Renaissance diagrams of the human body squaring the circle or providing templates for the classical orders take our own proportions as reliable measures of the harmony of the cosmos. So does the venerable parallel between the physical organization of ourselves and our buildings which should be, like us, bilaterally symmetrical according to a hierarchical system, which includes a head, trunk, limbs, peripheries, and even elements equivalent to intestines.

All these parallels are founded on the belief in a moral and spiritual order in the world which nowadays it would seem eccentric to maintain. Our more fragmented view is matched by quasi-architectural renditions of various parts of the body represented one by one in isolation.

Claes Oldenburg's modern colossi, architectural in scale but not in function, are always painfully literal and incomplete: the tunnel entrance in the form of a nose connects the slope of the nose-bridge with a cliff face, not with chin, cheekbones, and eye sockets. It is fairly plausible to match up the outline of a nose and a larger topographical incline, yet such assimilation is estranging as well.

Another Oldenburg proposal, the huge wading leg chopped off above the knee and stranded in the lower Thames, provokes other reflections. When has one ever seen a knee in isolation except in fragments of classical sculpture? It is a hallucination which focuses our attention unnaturally on an already overfamiliar feature of the world. A complete antique colossus would be easier to digest; even though it placed us differently, perhaps lower down, in the scale of creation, it would spring from a coherent inflated vision. Oldenburg's constructions, even when confined to small squares of paper, suggest alarming if amusing rents in the fabric of perception and reality.

He has eliminated a leg's main structural excuse: his leg holds up nothing. The legs on which Le Corbusier's Unité in Marseilles stands, more sensual versions of his famous pilotis or stilts, originally valued for releasing the ground under the building, have made it mobile and freed it from the earth to a degree. The basic geometry of the block remains rectilinear: personification goes only so far. Yet the slightest suggestion of this kind is so powerful that the idea of a complete colossus hovers above this building. It suggests that all supports of whatever size have something in common, thus linking the anatomy of cities and of persons, an underlying continuity which is not so far from the Renaissance theories.

A more bizarre and specialized correspondence between bodies and buildings was ordained in Ledoux's design for the House of Pleasure in his ideal city of Chaux in the forests of the Franche-Comté. This brothel-like institution was not to be tucked away in a back street but given a prominent public position and dignified porticoes. It not only accommodates but represents sexual urges, taking the form of a penis some hundreds of feet long. This message is most easily grasped in plan, which shows an oval salon surrounded by a portico at the end of a long shaft or corridor with small private rooms on either side, bulging out at the base into generous testicles containing parlors and galleries for dining.

Other parts of the great body formed by the whole architectural ensemble at Chaux are generally less literal: the head is abstract and there are no limbs. Ledoux's brothel gives a partial and inflexible representation of human sexuality, like an insignia or logo. The strong image is masked by the temple porch entrance, by the colonnade at the tip, by the massive podium on which it sits, and finally by a heavy rectangular mass piled on top of the body. As unruly passions are contained within it and forced to take part in a socially beneficial cleansing or plumbing, so the initially inflammatory idea is obscured by an architecture of received forms and phrases, and the excitement of the metaphor is drastically reduced.

Ledoux is nonetheless claiming the high authority of organic structure for his design, which seems also a motive at work in Calatrava's roof for a school assembly hall in Switzerland. Here we note an uncanny resemblance of the exposed support system in wood and concrete to human joints with their tendons in a different, softer material facilitating movement. In the school roof movement is notional only, but actual tensions are dramatized by the meeting of two different substances at the joint or pivot. So the resemblance to bodily arrangements, not slavishly exact, lends a kind of authenticity to this unlikely design.

Some of the most exuberant developments in Gothic vaulting have been given a similar derivation and interpreted as skeletal, articulated like the underlying structure of bones in a higher organism. But in later efflorescences of the style, at Sv. Borbora in the old Bohemian silver mining town of Kutná Hora for example, instead of bones the model seems to be the web of nerve fibers in the spine or brain, partly because elements seem to group themselves in one pattern and then in another, aligning differently with their neighbors according to changes in our perspective.

Some will see this as simply another way of expressing the most common view of the development from Romanesque to late Gothic. Earlier, Romanesque passageways remind one of the lower body: aisles are intestinal—dark and engulfing—surrounding one with a continuous fabric of the same material in slightly irregular blocks or cells; so that everything is one kind of tissue, stone. In this phase windows are high up and few. The builders rest content with sensations of enclosure, and attention is focused inward, even downward. Putting worshipers in touch with the spiritual means reminding them of very different features of reality and parts of the body than it does a couple of centuries later in the heyday of Gothic. Romanesque man is rooted in the earth and finds its and his own heaviness reassuring, not a burden he struggles to be free of.

Occasionally openings in buildings are explicitly linked to particular orifices of the body. Very exceptionally the whole building is treated as a human head, like the howling face at Bomarzo behind which is a room entered by the mouth lit by the eyes. More viable because stuck less rigidly in a single expression or mood are generalized organic orifices such as one finds in Louis Sullivan's bank at Grinnell, Iowa. This design is both sparing and lavish, with blank expanses of brickwork punctured dramatically (too high for a usable entrance) by a large round window which expands into circles set within squares and further squares rotated forty-five degrees. One could analyze this as a decorative motif and miss the point. The overlay converts the opening into living tissue which can focus like a lens or expand and contract like a muscle. As it occurs on the entrance facade of a bank we might wonder whether this is an eye or an anus, but the gorgeous fringe allows us to regard it as the multivalent opening on the world of something like a sea anemone.

More diffuse suggestions of architectural features as organic orifices set in surrounding flesh occur in gardens: springs or fountains when at all naturalized breed the fancy of the earth as a fecund body from which beneficial fluids flow. At Rousham in Oxfordshire the cascade is pillowed in rolling terrain, and one imagines oneself wandering over magnified bits of feminine anatomy and coming to rest cradled in a soft fold of the skin. The power of the analogy lies in its vagueness not its literalness, and also in our hazy reduction to something even smaller than child size.

When Salvador Dalí decided to reconstruct a bit of female anatomy as inhabitable space, he made an odd choice and built a walk-in version of Mae West's face in his museum at Figueras. But here we do not walk into the mouth to enter the skull cavity. Rather we cross the chin (a short flight of steps), sit down on the lips (a sofa), where we can admire the eyes (pictures on the wall) or look out through the hair (curtains framing the whole interior). The arrangements are absurdly literal and turned inside out.

In Elizabethan poetry the lover sometimes imagines himself a flea who can crawl over the beloved unnoticed and at will, making a detailed survey of her charms. Perhaps Dalí is thinking of similar violations: though the woman is treated as an imposing icon she ends up being fingered, violated, worn threadbare. What looks like a kind of worship paves the way after a short interval to desecration. Like poetical comparisons all the translations prove treacherous in practice: the lips are velvet, the nose (a fireplace) is porcelain, the hair satin of a color which suggests that it has been artificially lightened. In Dalí's hands the goddess is realized as a monster.

The conventional parallel between Christ's body on the cross and the church building with arms (or transepts) and a head (or chancel) is always more abstract than Dalí's in Figueras, yet anomalies have from time to time cropped up. Occasionally the chancel is not perfectly on axis with the nave, a tilt which echoes Christ's head wearily leaning in pictures of the Crucifixion. So this is known as a weeping chancel.

Using it as a pattern one might predict drooping transepts or a hole halfway down the left aisle (a spear wound, in the form of a specially prominent door or window). Occasionally cloisters are connected here and might represent a kind of discharge. Looking at almost any major church in plan one finds all sorts of distortions introduced, such as side chapels which throw the symmetry out, like growths or lesions disfiguring the divine body.

In *The City of God* St. Augustine extemporizes wonderfully on the church (its members) as the realized body of Christ in the world. Noah's ark becomes a type for the sojourning of this body in the alien place which is not its real home, made of wood like the cross though its true material is souls. The Scriptural dimensions of the ark correspond exactly to the proportions of the human frame, enlarged many times of course.

Some parallels are overarching, some comparatively trivial. Knitting them all together is no easy task, but perfect consistency would not necessarily reassure one any better than this jumble of hints and flashes. In our condition how can we possibly look for more than broken inklings? For a few instants we see the church as a body and then we lose it again. The builders have not meant it that way but were guided by an unseen hand, or if they did intend it they could only bring it to pass very imperfectly, which is another reminder of the vast distance separating us from true comprehension.

Human bodies were interred in and around churches, of course, so that the buildings which imitated a body also contained them. Occasionally the crypt or boneyard became so congested that extraordinary measures were taken to deal with the upsurge of human remains above the ground.

At Sedlec in Bohemia this happened around 1870 when an artist named Frantisek Rint was brought in to deal with these embarrassing riches and managed to turn them to decorative effect. So from imitating the body we pass to actually using parts of it to represent something else. Thus at Sedlec we find garlands of skulls with arm bones as spacers between the beads, and huge crowns and coats of arms and obelisks and flower arrangements all in bones. Perhaps the greatest tours de force are the no longer operative chandeliers, which are touted to contain every one of the 206 bones in the human body and which boast dangling fringes and sprays of stylized foliage not in gold braid or glass or wrought metal but in bleached bone.

memento mori

In the sixteenth century and before, skeletons were used to remind people of their mortality. But at Sedlec fripperies of bone work in an almost opposite sense, producing light-headed hilarity, not morbid reflectiveness. Perhaps we can never be entirely at ease here: replicas of everyday objects in bone aren't neutral the way models made of matchsticks are, though a case of similar persistence in using building blocks which are the wrong shape, color, and texture for what they represent.

Many sixteenth-century works of art depict a world made of bones in a less literal sense than the perverse underground universe at Sedlec. Paintings by Bosch and Bruegel showing saints tempted by devils, or cities overrun by demonic hordes, imply that the landscape is infested by bones as if the earth were a great body. So our position is like Jonah's in the whale, a small organism caught in a larger one. The conception of a whole world of correspondences where microcosm echoes macrocosm survives longest in negative form: one might disappear into the ravening maw at any moment.

Views of early Renaissance collectors' dens rationalize this perception so that walking into their tight-packed enclosures is like paying a visit to one of your own organs, where you are surrounded by bits of an undigested meal. Often the bits are chosen for indigestibility because one can't assimilate them according to any known coordinates, can't even decide whether they are animal or mineral, first course or dessert.

Like the Renaissance collectors Gaudí hung up his trophies, the famous pendulous models made of wire with many small bags of lead shot attached. After countless adjustments of these weights he got the shapes he wanted and the model was photographed and then inverted to give you a picture of the building. The theory of this odd type of model is that one is taking dictation from natural forces, so the final result will be an organic shape discovered not invented. But all the surviving examples suggest that although he employed the procedure to generate fresh ideas, he filtered very purposefully what it could tell him. The results are steep but symmetrical paraboloids: a unitary form emerges from many separate manipulations. Gaudí's notion of the organic depends on a high degree of irregularity within the rough parameters of the overall shape; thus porch supports in the Colonia Güell crypt are connected by ribs in patterns which sometimes approximate rows of interlocking triangles raying into hexagons. Gaudí differs from any conceivable Gothic model in the way he violates the nascently regular geometry. Nothing falls where you expect it, but the variations never seem arbitrary: the building's elements flex in sensitive muscular response to the pressures they meet. It is part of Gaudí's genius to know how far one can distort a grid and make it look like natural movement, not monstrous aberration. If it were plotted, one would find that deflection of columns and consequent twisting of ribs and bowing of roof surfaces was slight but continual. The building behaves like a living thing, and although its elements are fixed they depict a momentary response. Even a small twist in a member we regard as incapable of such flexibility gives us a shock like having the furniture come alive.

The flexibility in the forms is echoed in the textures. The roof of Casa Battló resembles a dragon's spine, with bulgy knobs which protect the joints on the ridge to represent vertebrae. The spine also shows itself in prongs or bumps, as if the skeleton were magnified outside the body by a larger shadow. Flanks on either side of this ridge are tiled differently, the outer one to the street in tougher scales, the inner one to the court in softer mosaic, a defensive as against a vulnerable skin.

Drawings of the facade show him overlaying different sorts of organic geometry which cannot add up to a single coherent scheme. The main logic of the window surrounds on the principal floors seems to be that of bones and cartilage. Near the glass, the flesh parts or falls away to reveal a bony substratum. Windows open like eyes, mouths, orifices without a name, or a condition in the flesh verging on putrefaction. But then the tops of the openings make ambiguous suggestions, borrowing something from the geometry of crystals.

Looking among traditional African mud architecture we find even more powerful instances of buildings conceived as bodies. Mosques in the Ivory Coast are collections of sentinel-like shapes in a substance like bread. The tops of the large peaked cones bristle with individual hairs or teeth which are the crosspieces of a wooden frame jutting through the fleshy covering. The clustered mounds remind us of Gaudí's parabolas, and in fact he flirted with such settings and forms in a proposal for a Franciscan mission in Tangiers. Here the towers are strong masses but have soft edges, which resemble the slopes left by a natural settling as of a sand dune or a mountain, reflecting both the method of construction and the process of weathering. The mosques are dripped into place to begin with and then gently washed away by the weather.

Even more startling versions of the building as a living thing, Dogon shrines in Mali have millet porridge offerings poured over them from the top downward, pouring which repeats and enlarges the earlier act of building. The food is usually lighter in color and smoother in texture than the clay but harder to distinguish from the substance beneath than the paint or gilding of European decoration. Occasionally such shrines have facelike facades, in which a mouth opening is framed by squat watchtowers surprisingly near the European two-towered format for a church facade. Food in this case is not placed near the mouth but painted onto the forehead and thus allowed to make maximum visual impact as well as increasing the building's substance with no waste. One can imagine cases where the adornments have overtaken the body underneath and significantly increased the size of the object by this feeding. The point is that the building grows and changes, consuming the provisions its devotees bring. The temple as itself

the god has become a metaphor in European religion, but here it
is several steps nearer to literal enactment, where participants treat
buildings as if you had to feed and tend them like persons.

Sources for the beguiling but inefficient forms of these cluster
buildings have been sought in the natural world. One author
matches pictures of the clump of mud spires and a large termites'
nest of unnervingly similar outline. But what does this seemingly
exact coincidence tell? The materials used are similar up to a point.
Mud almost inevitably ends up in soft sloping forms, but there the
resemblance ends, in the nature of the material and its reaction
to rain and gravity. Otherwise the comparison is less exact than
it looks, the nest accretive in an utterly different way from the
mosque. When one puts the two together because of the resemblance in their outlines, one is putting a city (the termite mound)
next to a single building (the mosque) and forgetting to adjust for
scale. The unsolved mystery is why the termites should build so
high instead of spreading along the ground, if not to escape flood-
ing or some other ground-hugging danger.

There are more profound though less startling links between
African buildings and natural forms; mountains, large boulders, and
the loose communities of plant species all seem to be picked up in
the shape and organization of human dwellings. Clustered mounds
turn up in unlikely materials. In northern Cameroon villages consist of little mountain ranges whose peaks are cones made of reeds,
where a labyrinth of peaked family precincts has a single entrance.
The profound effect of this crowding on social life would take years
to understand. The extended household is a single body and its inhabitants would have different ideas from ours about whether an
individual body and consciousness exist at all.

In the desert edge communities of Niger in central Africa the
most striking architecture to an outsider's eye is that of the large
millet granaries, sometimes collected in abandoned mud forts to

make them more easily defensible. There they form cities of jars, each one fixed in place and taller than a human figure. The spaces between are similar to but crucially different from intervals between inhabited buildings. You naturally imagine these spaces colonized by use, as if they were little half-enclosed courtyards for idling or working in, places to sit and watch passing traffic. In fact the gaps between have only one function, to allow access to the mouths of the granaries: users need to prop ladders on every one of the jars. Nonetheless the granaries seem to group themselves in meaningful families and leave the outsider imagining significance in the arrangements, which might include a historical series with ruined or obsolete examples in close proximity which are left up because it's tedious to take them down, but with a little of the effect of a ghost town. The nature of the structures means forms can be freer than in windowed rooms, like magnified pots or large simple animals, no more than plump sacks with heads and feet at a rudimentary stage of development.

In Nubian traditional dwellings, doorways give the best idea of what it is like to live in an earthen dwelling. The soft and before long slightly ragged edges make for a special intimacy with the substance of one's house. In these communities it is not uncommon to make entrances from the street a trial or ordeal, fringing them with teeth, larger than life-size and pinked out in clay, echoed by a crocodile skull stuck in the wet surface, with large eyes in the form of embedded china plates just beneath.

Carrying through such ideas, once inside you would be inhabiting a larger host, visiting its organs. Among the most visceral of all traditional interiors are the focal sofas of Turkey, central sitting spaces from which the more specialized rooms branch off. At the edge of the Turkish sofa or connecting room is a smaller alcove, a kind of pouch thrown out from the main mass. It is generally raised one step and partly closed off by an open railing. It is often lit by the only windows in the room, which means that it draws the eyes and attention. The alcove is more thickly carpeted than the larger space, and around three sides of it runs a low seat covered in carpets and cushions.

Entering this alcove, one is penetrating by stages to smaller and more richly padded spaces. The ritualized layout of the alcove in the sofa, with its seat-ledge, integral with the fabric and a way of inhabiting the wall, derives from the nomad's organization of the tent. Walls and floors are hung or covered in carpets; sacks of clothing, bedding, and other gear lined up around the perimeter become seating or backrests when covered with carpets. So the stationary urban sofa refers back to an even more organic space, clothed throughout in soft woven patterns and arranged in a sweeping curve.

The most fantastic nonvernacular venture into the visceral was made by the German Expressionist architect Hermann Finsterlin, though none of his buildings resembling magnified tumors or other diseased tissue were ever built. More plausible though still short-lived attempts at an architecture organic at a molecular level occurred early this century in Czechoslovakia.

The most striking thing about Czech Cubist architecture is that there are no bland or normal, almost no flat, bits of the fabric. The building's whole substance is tense with activity, which shows in faceted three-dimensional play on all surfaces. At its shallowest this is a kind of decorative patterning of the facade. Even the most radical examples are organized symmetrically with little sense of the violent assault on reality found in Picasso's earliest Cubist works.

Surfaces are broken into facets not to suggest centrifugal forces but to depict a connectedness which is nearer the structure of organisms than of buildings. Thus the messages we get about structure from Czech Cubism are misleading in a practical sense, and depict a metaphoric unity which has been imposed theoretically. The designers have willed a change in the nature of architecture which does not go as far as structure. Thus they provoke comparison with rococo, another architecture of disguise and rampant illusion.

Perhaps the very short life of Cubism in architecture is explained by its metaphoric character. The new identity for buildings remains ingenious intellectual clothing. It is most powerful viewed myopically, that is to say when one focuses on the play of shadow around hubs or meeting points on a facade. Then the light falling on deep indentations in the surface makes a rippling like complicated muscle structure glimpsed beneath the skin, and for a moment it seems a valid way of animating architecture.

These buildings *represent* organic life forms, while Scharoun's designs for certain public institutions—schools above all—are powerfully shaped by them, not embodying but responding to organic form. The deepest level of such organization is found in the plans, which seem to grow and change before our eyes. They are ungainly to a degree, with strange organs and protrusions which have developed in response to peculiarities of the environment. Only such ideas of growth will account for these eccentric conglomerates, which join clusters of individual cells by means of irregular common spaces which are corridors one minute, indoor squares the next, and then throw out further little private corners. The whole arrangement is organic not through literal imitation of organisms but because this nervous flexibility is devoted to accommodating life, more a stimulus to it than an image of it, anticipating and shaping its rhythms. It holds out an ideal of fluent unfolding, diverging, meeting—development which ebbs and then hurries forward—intensely subjective but supported by the continual presence of others. Scharoun's is an antigeometrical understanding, nearer in plan to an African village than to the ideal cities of the Renaissance.

In classical systems of proportion the human figure is the generating motif in a more literal and easily traceable way. Scharoun derives his irregular plans from a certain conception of bodily *function* or *activity*, whereas the classical system in a designer like Palladio, say, derives from bodily *proportion*. The body underlies the scaling and disposition of architecture, and then at a certain point resurfaces again as a visible marker or measuring device which makes spaces meaningful or at least more readily comprehensible.

One of the most purely iconic and rhetorical occurrences is also one of the most painfully literal. Instead of a figure pressed into holding up a building this is a column which supports a figure, St. Simeon Stylites isolated on his high perch. The plan of his monastery near Antioch shows that the ascetic escaping the world was converted shortly after his death from a lonely monument in the desert to a social focus, around which clustered a series of churches. He remains the visible reason they face the way they do, and, represented by his column, is converted to a prominent object of contemplation, a living work of architecture adorning a public space.

Human proportions in a more subliminal form lie beneath everything Palladio did. A surprising fragment in Vicenza reveals features of his method which he never meant us to see. This is the Palazzo Porto Breganze, of which only two bays (of a projected seven or nine) were built. The result is a surrealist monster whose giant order looks impossibly tall because undiluted by the intended horizontal spread. The fragment throws into stark relief the overlay of two entirely different scales in this design: normal human needs are set against the giant order, and our dimensions understood by inventing an enormous race whose grandeur the columns would match. Palladio has enlarged a classical order sufficiently to fit a row of windows into the entablature and a series of even larger openings into the column bases. These make a travesty of the original meanings of these components and cause a drastic realignment of perception. Horizontal divisions on the wall between the columns create the impression that a different smaller building has been trapped behind. He often plays this way with incompatible (though harmonically related) scales, which suggest two orders of beings, us and an outlandish ideal.

Sometimes in rural projects like the Villa Capra, his adherence to rectangular ideas of habitable space gives way in the great cylindrical centerpiece, like a sculptural head set in the landscape and merged via angular connectors to the rest of the building which is not curved. The most telling sign of an underlying organicism here is Palladio's integration of house, outbuildings, and landscape via graded magnitudes, and the occasional presence of figural sculpture which he uses to measure larger and more distant features.

Grander if more elusive correspondences are sometimes attempted: whole settlements have based themselves on the human form. In Crete the plan of the town of Gourniá is said to derive from female anatomy. Modern maps make this hard to pick out, suggesting that one might easily pay a substantial visit and pace the streets without realizing that one was traversing the limbs and organs of a presiding spirit of the place.

Less ambitious in its literal mimicry and therefore easier, Litomyšl in Czechoslovakia presents a simple example of an organically inspired plan focused on a single long, thin public space. This arcaded square, which widens at both ends, contracts in the middle to something like normal street width. It curves unemphatically throughout, partially obscuring a view of one end from the other and making the whole length an unfolding progress which cannot be grasped all at once.

The sense of uneven density as one traverses its length, of being circulated through a system by mild squeezing pressure, invites one to retraverse this route, learning it by absorption rather than analysis. It is the greatest triumph of an organic, nonrational organization that the subordinate parts, which all lie north of the central thread, are thoroughly joined to it and read with reference to it. These include churchyards and neglected courts in front of pompous buildings, which at Litomyšl become dependencies or adjuncts of the street of shops. How such an organism grows in the first place remains imperfectly understood. Hundreds of small choices over a lengthy span result finally in a style of organization which resembles in a few striking ways the physical structure of its creators.

4 Landscape

Landscape can be a neutral ground, a foil or contrary principle, or a more profound source whose energies might be tapped by the architect. Before the eighteenth century it would not have been a subject, or at least not a positive one. Brief mentions from Shakespeare's time show that landscapes which seem magnificent to us, like the Lake District, were to them horrid wastes to be endured, which conjured up visions of bandits and violence.

More recently the subject has become urgent through an increase in the scale of architecture, and through overpopulation, though this last is perhaps problematic, at least in our part of the world, and sometimes just means more people than you are used to.

In such a misanthropic mood, one looks for a landscape free of the human presence. If there is always something paradoxical about such a search—one has to wish oneself out of the picture even as one enjoys it—in England the hope is always semi-imaginary. Even Wastwater, the wildest lake in the Lake District, must be edited to seem truly wild. Almost any vantage point includes sheep tracks as well as forbidding screes, and one must turn one's back on the road running within a few hundred yards of the shore. Besides, it is hard to suppress the thought as one contemplates the unscalable screes that they are the waste from an unknown industrial process. Dingy gray and regular in form, they are a kind of natural waste, thrown down by a more inscrutable activity than mining.

But one only has to be left alone in this kind of landscape for a short time to look round for reassurance, which can be provided by a Mars Bar wrapper or a jar in Tennessee or a single cabin in a vast forest or by the dotted signs of human intellect which go to make up a work by an artist like Robert Smithson. Order need only be intimated by a slender focal feature for the wanderer to extrapolate from it half consciously until the whole visual field is subtly altered by human intention.

Dry stone walls have sometimes been held up as examples of deeply rooted human artifacts, close to natural process: they follow the contours of the land and their coursing adopts a wave rhythm which resembles geological strata. But the real purpose of these dry stone walls, like the earliest human writing, is to establish accurate property lines. They mark out what belongs to whom without the necessity of a human presence to enforce it, and like most birdsong are attractive ways of saying "this is mine; don't come in."

An even more minimal and idealized human presence is established by the Saxon and Celtic crosses that survive in peripheral and underinhabited parts of England and Wales. These are territorial too in their way, points extended upward a number of feet, which mark the spot where a preacher stood and would stand, and function as a surrogate figure to remind you of him when he is gone. Often they were decorated, like a cope, with tiers of smaller figures in priestly robes, a set of symbols which would need unraveling like a sermon.

These constructions are among the most discreet of physical symbols, but sometimes the presence of a building is more completely camouflaged and only indicated by the larger natural feature which masks it, like the clump of ancient yews which cluster round the little church at the top of Wastwater. Once you know what you are looking at, the dark smudge at the foot of Great Gable represents the church, embodied in a ring of living things.

Sometimes buildings are even mistaken for natural formations. Coming across the troglodytic dwellings of Cappadocia one might imagine that they grew that way like coral, and earthquakes and the disinhabiting which follows have contributed to this impression, but in fact the way this partly found architecture came about is almost the reverse of this imagined process.

The cells were made, not found or grown. Rooms aren't a natural occurrence here, and the fact that we could think they are is a tribute to the accidental camouflage caused by the deterioration of the rock. Its softness, which makes usable shapes easy to obtain, also makes them easy to lose. Hence the "naturalness" of these complexes, like mellow eruptions of the soil. But people only live in caves in Jacobean court masques, in psychoanalytic narratives, and in poverty-stricken backwaters.

Vernacular building, like landscape, does not come in truly individual forms. It is always generic and instances of it can therefore be chosen at random. Take almost any eighteenth-century farmhouse in the Aveyron, with walls of local fieldstone from which a coat of render has fallen away. A stair and a raised walkway pass along the front of the building, above the lower ranges meant for animals, before coming to rest in a knotted corner where roofs converge. Out of the back side of the main wing sticks the bread oven like a little stone apse. The roofs descending at different angles are made of stone slates with the strange name *lauzes*, carefully graded from large to small.

This house has knitted itself into its outbuildings and an adjoining farmyard in an even more derelict state than its own. The sensation of buildings growing out of the soil is enhanced by lack of care amounting more and more to ruin. Passageways crooked to begin with become more obscure by growing partway shut. Now that the stair up to it is broken in half, the paneled rococo door still showing traces of gray paint looks even more like elegance strayed in from somewhere else.

One can't be sure if this farmhouse looks so natural because of a slow accretive mode of growth, deep conservatism in the forms to begin with, or simply the lack of fresh paint, touches of which would be enough to undo the gradual process by which everything approximates to the same color, a mousy gray-brown.

As in other humble products, some of the most enchanting signs are faint apings of grander things, like the shallow stone arches in barn openings, window surrounds, and the crude arcade under the raised walkway, features perhaps at bottom Roman.

In studied derivatives of French rural building like Marie Antoinette's artificial hamlet on the outskirts of Versailles, such sophistications poke through less unexpectedly. She envies the naturalness of traditional buildings, which belong where you find them like wildflower seeds that have rooted where they fell, so she commissions a painter and a theatrical designer to make her something like the villages she has passed through. The Queen's House in her hamlet has the typical outside gallery for reaching the human quarters over the beast ones, except that its spindly stilts convey that it is craning for the view. Underneath is the dairy where court ladies milked cows into silver pails and made butter on marble counters, while above at gallery level is the ballroom which provided relief from these made-up chores.

Among many urban derivatives of rustic buildings is the savage castle Mark Twain built himself in Hartford on the huge earnings from his tales of simple people in remote backwaters, often conveyed in outlandish country dialect, the linguistic equivalent of patterned brickwork and timber framing. Like Marie Antoinette's hamlet, Twain's house sports a colorful variety of materials and is wreathed in wooden porches which give strangely Japanese views of his tame suburban lawns.

In this whole regressive tradition some of the most successful camouflages are British. At Bedales, the progressive school in Hampshire, Ernest Gimson built a library very much like a barn, with an exposed roof of curved timbers and haylofts into which he fit some bookshelves. Was it an attempt to naturalize learning, or an even more Philistine effort to make students restive and send them out into the fields in search of healthier activities than reading?

Gimson pushed to another extreme of forced naturalism at Stoneywell Cottage, a house he built for his brother in Charnwood Forest in Leicestershire. The effect he wanted here is conveyed much better by a contemporary woodcut than by photographs, which show the humiliations that fires in the thatch and hankerings after convenience have administered to this building.

Gimson's woodcut concentrates on the chimney, a piece of stonework which resembles a small cliff face. The boundary between the building and its setting is blurred and the number of stories is obscured by a change of level near the chimney which leaves a little figure stranded on a pinnacle opposite a first-floor window. In this small project Gimson has got rid of clear edges and consistent levels, a short flight from rationality which leaves one living in a house like a misshapen boulder.

In early garden suburbs like Bedford Park the vocabulary is different but a number of intentions are the same. Bedford Park is built of red brick trimmed in white wood. At the beginning hedges were not allowed, only white picket fences, which doesn't sound very primitive or even rural but corresponds to a certain vision of innocence, harking back to a simpler time almost two centuries earlier. In spite of its Dutch gables the mode is defiantly English and unsophisticated, one of the earliest essays in vernacular revival.

By its small scale and the irregular layout of dusty lanes it brought a countrified existence to arty types, many of whom worked in the City. The extension of suburban railways determined its location, and the station provides the clue to how Bedford Park could be kept so parklike, free of up-to-date industry and commerce. It fed on London, with only the barest sign of this relation.

The American equivalent of Bedford Park is not instantly recognizable. Forest Hills in Queens looks much more like the Seven

Dwarfs than Queen Anne, deriving its architectural vocabulary from medieval Germany. In the public buildings, which include an inn and town hall, incinerators terminate in witch's hats, roofs are organic humps, and pedestrian bridges look like Gothic fortifications. In spite of such outlandish clothing the ideology is exactly that of Bedford Park, a protected realm swarming with greenery and dotted with archaic miniature castles, on the doorstep of a large dirty metropolis.

Despite the fact that the tradition of picturesque disguise has many living descendants, it has proved in a broad sense sterile, through placing strict limits on what landscape is allowed to mean. Its ideal is to plant houses artfully in a large garden- or parklike space; but even its conception of a garden is flattened and sanitized.

Treated more freely, the history of gardens can reinvigorate the relation between architecture and its natural surroundings. Continental gardens of the seventeenth or eighteenth century often realize architectural forms in plants. At the Casa del Campo near Celorico de Basto in northern Portugal, a whole range of structures are imitated in hedge, and although one knows better, one can't help feeling that the devices of the architect have been ratified by the natural world and appear as spontaneous growths. Rather than a deformation of the development proper to plants, it seems an invitation to human builders to experiment with new links between building and growth.

At Chiswick House in London hedge corridors extend as far as the eye can see, in forms borrowed from but purer than architecture, because relieved of the necessity to open out in rooms. In a house, corridors for their own sake would make no sense; in a garden, the contrary is true: forms which do nothing give the greatest satisfaction. No architectural interior can approach the perfect metaphysical emptiness of the round roomlike space which houses the rotunda in the garden at Chiswick. A round building sits beside a round pond ringed by trees in round tubs, a place elemental and symbolic. It embodies a myth of the center which if taken too literally will have you diving into the pool to plumb its imaginary depths.

A garden is at bottom the strongest of symbolic configurations. There are gardens which are little more than a perimeter wall, like the Casa de Simães at Moura in Portugal with a main gate like a Chinese pavilion in flimsiest silhouette and Baroque curlicues along the top edge like stylized growth. This wall is an archetype of the boundaries set by art, paper-thin but too high to see over. Inside this derelict garden the little which remains is generated by the wall, from which growth spills and fountains dribble. Only a rudimentary framework survives, but it conveys all the more the power that inheres in this contrast of nature and culture, which takes us by surprise in the back view of the main gate. This view with small wooden flaps in the stone frame was not especially meant to be seen, but the encounter gives the purest glimpse of the division into two worlds and the secrecy of the one we are in.

The typical eighteenth-century garden draws a clear boundary between itself and its house, which does not insinuate itself into the garden but offers a flat facade like a theater backdrop which may be, as at Queluz, strewn with plant motifs in plaster, the whole thing colored pink and green in distant acknowledgment of hedges and the soil. Toward the end of the century more impinging clashes occur, and we find landscapes erupting in or bursting through architecture. At Ledoux's Hôtel Thélusson in Paris, demolished in the nineteenth century, a chaste classical villa is introduced by a half-buried triumphal arch in harshly rusticated stonework. In between the entrance and the house is a bombshell, a romantic garden hidden from the street because below the level of the entrance floor. It is like a cave or grotto which has thrust its way to the surface from under the house and now lies half exposed to view. Architecture sits uneasily astride chaotic forces which it can't entirely suppress.

A similar process occurs within doors in John Soane's London house. At the heart of this dwelling is a tube of empty space at the bottom of which rests an Egyptian sarcophagus, as if Soane has dug down in the London clay and found a strange intruder. The disquieting presence is located within, so here, as in Gothic novels, one does not flee from but cultivates one's horrid secrets. It can be taken for granted that interesting psyches contain narrow passages, dank depths, and unlovely encrustations. Architecture and self-knowledge are like archaeology, and one way of describing the interesting new mysteries one detects in one's explorations is to say that one has uncovered a landscape indoors, that some interior spaces are as wild as any heath.

There is a twentieth-century Italian designer who likes to present his results as if he found them by digging, as if they were there and he uncovered them. Many of Carlo Scarpa's earlier projects were renovations or conversions of historic buildings, even, in the case of the most famous, the Castelvecchio in Verona, structures it was possible to present as ruins.

Scarpa's method is to inhabit the building by interpreting it to itself in modern idiom, using the new materials as if they occurred on site. Juxtapositions of textures suggest the passage of time—his slow and reflective method makes itself felt as an analogue of the longer processes of history which have washed over the ground.

Scarpa's favorite stepped or zigzag molding suggests peeling off successive layers, revealing older stages which lie beneath the surface. There is also the whittled edge that might seem decorative in intention but is another sign of fraying—not decay but an organic softening of simpler human geometry. Clear first thoughts are complicated by revision, which is felt to be kin to forces which operate on landscape, and many of Scarpa's familiar forms give pictures of weathering.

The Olivetti showroom in Venice is an exquisite version of a peeling facade, while the Brion family cemetery at San Vito d'Altivole is a collection of mysterious fragments from a forgotten rite. There he built from scratch the kind of archaic world which had been the preexistent given in other projects. For Scarpa, who likes to draw hints out of the ground or suggest meanings which lie too deep for full exposure, the idea of a cemetery has a special resonance.

At San Vito the reconciliation of cultural forms to landscape is expressed in a variety of ways. Many elements are exquisite but at the same time incomplete. Walls break off leaving a ragged edge, more like a Japanese screen or sliding panel than the fortified perimeter which, within their moat, they seemed at first. Water is a powerful but ambiguous presence throughout, at times suggesting immobility or torpor, and hence acceptance. Contrarily, when we come to the graves, a stylized rivulet animates them with its subdued current.

The tomb forms are perplexing. Neither indoors nor outdoors, sheltering under a kind of bridge which makes a gentle mound but lifts itself free of the ground, the tomb slabs slope toward each other and a meeting somewhere in the air above, which hasn't happened yet. It is a built landscape offering its obscure analogues to familiar natural features in concrete, tile, glass, and bronze. Though the rituals are not insistent and the symbols are cloudy, who can doubt that Scarpa is expressing a mystical creed, especially here where his subject death so naturally invites it?

Though Alvar Aalto is much nearer to the mainstream of modernism, he feels from early in his career a need for more open, less determinate orders than strict modernism seems to allow, and, like Scarpa, he looks to landscape to suggest them. The most powerful indicator of a new kind of organization at the Villa Mairea of 1938–1939 is the plan, which strings together elements in a rectilinear pattern suggesting an organic spiral. At one end of this limblike arrangement is the main house, and at the other is a sauna and pool. In between is a space which the building gathers up and half encloses as with an encircling arm.

The architectural vocabulary changes radically as we move from one end to the other, from elegant white geometry modulating through curved timber facing to the rustic sauna roofed with sod. This is not just a stylistic gamut but the continuum in the inhabitants' lives between one realm and another. The plan expresses a certain reconciliation between man and nature, indoor and outdoor, sophisticated and primitive. So the borrowings from traditional structures operate in the service of a serious attempt at an integrated existence.

In a larger public project of a dozen years later, the civic center at Säynätsalo, Aalto practices an even subtler naturalism. The rhythms of the building seem to take their cues from accidental groupings of trees in the vicinity, not a secure basis for permanent architecture, since trees die and cannot be incorporated in architectural compositions one by one (in fact a series could be assembled of twentieth-century structures built around particular trees which later proved uncooperative).

Aalto's reliance on the randomness of tree groupings is sufficiently generalized not to be threatened by the disappearance of a few specimens. To cut down the whole surrounding forest or see it fall victim to disease would of course seriously denude Aalto's buildings, which are full of analogues to the forest—like the openwork passageways of timber which cause light to dapple, or uprights in an interior court which line up with the trunks of the trees outside.

The most startling transposition between architecture and nature worked in this complex is a stairway grassed and planted until it almost disappears, which provides an escape from the attempted enclosure of the courtyard. Here architecture and landscape have changed places and the latter obeys the more rigorous geometry and performs the more useful work, knitting up separated arms of the brick structure. In its gentle way this stair is as powerful as one of those early Cubist compositions in which trees and teacups have a similar value, so that it would be hard to say which showed more thought, or which was more natural, because all substance is unified here by strong perception.

Even such pronounced acts of shaping can look mild and recessive beside the more assertive work of Frank Lloyd Wright. Fallingwater, a famous example of a building in a landscape, has sometimes been seen as a building dominating a landscape. Wright's clients had asked for a house in one of their favorite picnic spots with a good view of the waterfall in Bear Run. But instead of meekly facing this landscape feature, Wright perched his building atop it so that the water runs through the house, which throws out a series of cantilevered shelves like an abstract code for rock formations.

Photographed from underneath, Wright's design can look like a crass imposition on a wild place. But it is a strong architectural assertion whose heavy mass comes apart into horizontal flakes which project themselves independently in different directions. Inside, one finds that the structure which seemed from afar to be all concrete and glass has a masonry core. At the center are cave-like depths and a hearth where the underlying rock seems to push its way through the level floor. Internal spaces are negatives of the rock shelves, flat slices of air held between a stone floor and an overhanging ledge, the ceiling.

This building has been compared to a Chinese garden hut or a Japanese tea pavilion but is more melodramatic than they and bolder in inventing new structures to express architecture's integration with the natural world. Though not literally imitative in its forms, it has an aim no Oriental building could understand, to be physically inseparable from the landscape.

Tea pavilions in the grounds of the Katsura Palace in Kyoto go further in some ways than any Western structure to open architecture to its natural surroundings, which are not untouched woodland as in Pennsylvania but carefully composed gardens with lakes, islands, and little forests. The Japanese buildings are remarkably ready to let in views and breezes, to vacate almost entirely until they become little more than flimsy platforms from which one contemplates and to a degree suffers the weather.

Every enclosing wall of the building has been reduced to a paper-thin membrane which acts as the most minimal filter of sensations coming in from outside. So insubstantial and retiring are these edges that one easily loses any consciousness of them.

Many details in the surrounding terrain, and especially the paths, show sophisticated tolerance of disorder no Western art can match. Yet this is not the whole story. Randomness in Japanese landscape is always carefully selected. A straight-edged, mortared stone path breaks down into a wild scattering of single flags, but there are principles at work even here, as shown by the sparseness of the stepping stones—it is simply that the logical mind can't entirely comprehend them.

Conventional elements of the tea ceremony regularly appear in naturalistic disguise. Thus the water basin may be a hollowed rock like an old stump, polished smooth somewhere else, by the sea or a fast-running river. A museum of textures is hidden in this outdoor corner, invisible to the ignorant. The confident Japanese understanding of natural process produces a result like spontaneity or disorder, founded on rigorous selection.

For Western parallels to this degree of control, one must turn to French formal landscapes like the one which filled the space between Cardinal Richelieu's chateau and his elegant little planned town, an arrangement which can now be studied only in contemporary bird's-eye views. Admittedly the scale and emptiness of this exercise would be abhorrent to a Japanese observer. Nothing could be further from their taste than such vast, symmetrical sameness. Yet in the desire to impose meaningful pattern and to see it operate through a carefully graded hierarchy of forms, the two cultures overlap.

These obsessive overorderings of landscape in the name of art are by no means an expired tradition. Bernard Tschumi's plan for the Parc de La Villette provides an up-to-date example. The guiding principle of this project is the overlay of discordant or at least noncongruent systems. Tschumi starts with a large irregular tract on the outskirts of Paris which has a history and a minimal geology. These are ignored or defied, and the ground is ruled off methodically according to an orthogonal grid. The points arrived at this way will turn out to be the sites for a series of pavilions or follies. Overlaid on this are various meandering arrangements inspired by the up-to-date medium of film.

The follies owe something to eighteenth-century landscape gardens, but Tschumi's little temples are not naturalized, quite the reverse, being derived from the heartless manipulation of an elementary geometry into a forced variety and then painted bright red. He studiously avoids atmosphere or aura throughout; this is an unashamedly mental landscape, the gigantic embodiment of ideas. Disparate particles are animated or connected up diagrammatically by elevated walkways with rippling awnings and sloping supports to convey the fluid consciousness instigated by film.

Though quintessentially disjointed, Tschumi's work shares with Libera's Villa Malaparte on Capri the conception of landscape as a ground waiting to be dominated by culture. Libera's villa is a more traditional and flamboyant imposition of alien geometry on, this time, a much more resistant topography.

He has plumped down an undiluted strong form on a promontory. Wright said one should never build on the top of a hill but on the brow, so one was effectively both on and under the natural eminence. Not a rule that Libera has observed: he puts a mountain on a mountain. From the air his building looks like a large ramp leading to a view of the sea. The slope of the roof forms a set of railless steps, widening to a roof platform, flat and empty with only the sky visible as one ascends. It is a building featureless like the sea which lies in front of it, rather than craggy like the rocks it sits on. Though this is architecture which gives a strong sense of being in a particular place, it would perhaps never grow into a comfortable sensation, like remaining suspended indefinitely in a parachute, which may have suited Malaparte's military fantasies.

After the Second World War Frank Lloyd Wright produced a number of designs which set up a more grandiose relation to natural features than his earlier work. In Sea Cliff, another house named like Fallingwater for its setting, like Libera he takes an untenable position and holds it. This unbuilt design of 1945 outdoes the natural promontory by building a more aggressive one in concrete, giving a ship's prow to a continent. In another proposal, for a resort jutting into a large meteor crater in Arizona, he positions himself at the edge of an enormous geographical feature and is inflated by his proximity. Now he pits architecture against the greatest forces in the world and imagines winning.

Extreme natural situations evoked a vulgar response from the late Wright, whose idea of the architect's place in the universe had swollen uncontrollably. Extreme recent responses sometimes take their cue from disjointed terrain and amplify the conflicting signals sent out by the landscape to produce a design full of discords. In plan the Igualada Cemetery in Barcelona by the Spanish team of Miralles and Pinós looks like a game of pick-up sticks. The architects respond to a steep site by setting up countereddies which break up the easy flow of the ground. The frenetic quality of this spatial organization has its equivalent in projects intended for flat urban settings, where we interpret the agitation as expressing a particular view of the city, one that places high value on the natural incoherence of large social conglomerates.

The restlessness in Peter Salter's quirky structures is less evident than in these hyperactive Spanish works and resides more in how they sink back into the landscape than in how they initially stick out of it. Most remarkable is his responsiveness to certain features of the site which are not easily visible. His Osaka folly takes major cues from natural rhythms of the surroundings or accidental happenings in materials, which are in an obvious sense chosen and in another sense imposed on him by the place.

The use of local soil of sometimes strange and often unpredictable hues to form perimeter walls at Osaka is like turning up the ground and then studying its return to where it came from. This odd form of cultivation tolerates the eroding and degrading of its components—metal, wood, and clay—at different speeds, making the building a clock or measuring device which has brought the landscape to consciousness and made some of its features perceptible for the first time. Of course the Osaka project was planned from the start as a temporary structure—for a garden festival—so the drama of architecture overtaken by insidious forces which lurk in any setting has a special fitness. Yet even in such situations not every architect's response is to make an entertaining spectacle of his building's demise at the hands of the weather.

In this designer's more permanent proposals we would expect to find this same impulse to unite the building more than iconographically with natural process, in order to absorb lessons for which he is prepared to pay a good deal in practical terms. To how many architects would it be positively appealing that heavy snowfalls made their building inaccessible for seven months of the year, a building whose being is substantially devoted to the passage of this snow in melted form through its own innards, a drama that few of its users will ever see? So this resting place for climbers in the mountains near Kamiichi in Toyama prefecture in Japan has its fulfillment in a communion between architecture and nature from which an actual human presence is mainly excluded. This thoughtful little building is the nearest architectural thing to the tree falling in the forest with no one to hear it, except that in this case the designer prepares the event and knows roughly when it is happening.

In the whole category of grotesque and exaggerated responses to landscape Gaudí stands out. His early design for a suburban villa in Barcelona, the Casa Vicens, creates a repulsive tropical species from unlikely materials like machine-made ceramic tiles and jagged stepped forms. One can appreciate the lurid vegetable inspiration of this work best from old photographs showing the garden facade embowered in palms and other exotic growths from which it rises like their more articulate expression.

Throughout his career but most literally at the beginning Gaudí gravitates to bizarre and even threatening natural forms, prickly plants and animals defended by protruding prongs or horns. The gateposts of the Finca Güell are like a controlled thicket of briars at the top, rich, impacted, and a little dangerous. The juxtaposition of thorns and flesh is an image which never lost its force for Gaudí. In a much later work for the same patron, the chapel at Colonia Güell, window grilles made of discarded needles from the Güell textile mills are set in soft stonework, which forms a protective gristly rim like an ear around the glass and metal that has forced an opening in it.

The suggestions of movement for which Gaudí's buildings are so notable are frequently sinister. Standing under the famous series of inclined columns at the Parc Güell one can remind oneself of the structural logic of this unsettling arrangement, but one's senses cry out that the world is toppling and that it is madness to stay where one will soon be crushed.

For a vivid depiction of a universe inhabited by the unpredictable negative energy inhering in trees and cloud shapes as well as human beings, one cannot do better than the work of Gaudí's Russian contemporary the illustrator Ivan Bilibin. Both have their links with turn-of-the-century decadence and Art Nouveau but neither is a standard interpreter of those conventions. Bilibin's special contribution is to unearth hallucinatory menace in folk pattern—most vivid in heaps of dying warriors or the old crone Baba Yaga flying through a mushroom-infested forest brandishing an uprooted tree.

The architectural tradition of nightmare naturalism would include Bruce Goff, whose weird hybrids often veer toward the sinister, a kind of talking architecture which twists its face into leering expressions it is hard to escape. In the Bavinger house the gnarled stonework held in place by its thicket of wires is dotted with rough lumps of glass like eyes set deep in wrinkled flesh. There is at least one other pole in Goff's work: besides this naturalism red in tooth and claw he perpetrates enormous playthings—houses as spaceships or spinning tops or rows of silos. Whether this is a different fantasy world or the same, both belong to a sinister grown-up comic book.

The most powerful modern example of a demonic landscape is the space where the wall stood between East and West Berlin, which in the present interregnum forms a nowhere you can walk in. This desert at the center of a great city signifies a number of things including a horrific past: Hitler's bunker forms a hump among other low humps which break the monotony of the ground. No marker identifies the exact spot, so this evil influence spreads vaguely over the empty terrain.

The rubble here may date from 1945 or from the destruction of the Wall (by then only twenty-eight years old) in 1989. The ground is almost featureless except for the orderly lampposts and useless roads of paranoid suspicion. In spite of or because of this desolation, this swath of empty space between Potsdamer Platz and the Brandenburg Gate forms the most moving memorial to the human bleakness of the well-named Cold War. In the next phase the void is to be occupied by capitalist monsters. One can only hope that the new developments will sleep uneasily on their twice-desecrated ground.

No ideological boundary cuts through abandoned Apollo launch sites in Florida, but like the other no-man's-land in Berlin this flat terrain is littered with unwanted bits of technological hardware. Constructed at vast expense and used once, these places are paradigms of waste and help persuade one, not quite rationally, of the human uselessness of space flight as it is now conceived.

For an antidote to such dehumanized places where man shows himself an unfit inhabitant of the earth, we could turn to archetypally humanized spaces like the canals and squares of Venice where even the land is *built*. Always cognizant of the limitations placed on them by the surrounding water, the builders of this city have contrived an integration of all its parts which gives it the deep consistency of a landscape.

The other landscape is indoors. When Hans Scharoun approached the dead heart of Berlin, he found unconquerable desolation all around him. In the Philharmonie, built near the bomb-flattened center of the old city, he turns inward. The concert hall consists of eleven plots like small fields on a hillside, so the audience is broken into subgroups which are raised above and tilted toward each other like a collection of family domains. Scharoun called them vineyards and imagined the valley which they form covered by a cloud-tent. Considered as architectural spaces these are relatively grand, but remembering their moral ambitions they are a modest and reasonable attempt to regenerate our friendly home the earth in an alien time and place.

5

Models

At first glance this may seem an excessively specialized topic, focused as it is on one of the deficiencies of architecture, an art which must finally be executed at such a scale that it is impractical to construct trial versions at full size. Viewed negatively, models are crutches for ignorant clients and other poor visualizers who can't understand the building from plans or sections and need to be helped along with more literal forms.

But against such a dismissive view could be cited architects like Frank Gehry and Coop Himmelblau who design through models, which are thus exploratory and not just explanatory. And there are the extra-architectural meanings of miniature forms, which alert us to uses transcending function of this condensing act, and suggest that it is a mental operation of far-reaching consequence.

Model has two main senses: the first is a trial version, at a smaller scale, of something which does not yet exist or perhaps can never fully exist. This also includes post-versions, copies on a different scale in different materials of objects existing or no longer existing. The second use, as in "model child" or "model dwelling," is a metaphorical extrapolation from the first, which has lost or dropped the idea of a change of scale but imagines a world full of patterns for imitation.

Without stretching the concept unduly you could say that many existing buildings are models in the first sense, because they suggest greater scales or ambitions than were actually allowed to them: they remain miniatures of their true selves. Among these are works of Lutyens and Le Corbusier, and centralized churches of the Renaissance. This meaning can overlap with the metaphorical sense, the utopian dream, a category even children's toys sometimes inhabit. Thus this supposed practical tool easily becomes the vehicle of grand intentions.

A remarkable watercolor shows all Soane's works built and unbuilt crammed into a large room and brings out the miracle of models, which can put the whole world in a small space. Here houses, tombs, and large public projects are depicted as models of different sizes or as framed pictures hanging on or propped against walls. Their relations to each other constantly violate reality—Mrs. Soane's tomb is shown larger than the Tyringham gateway right behind it, a similar form. But this painting only depicts in more congested format what Soane does throughout the house in which the picture hangs. The smallest space, his dressing room, is crowned with a miniature replica of the lantern proposed for a grand stair in the House of Lords. The picture room with movable walls keeps expanding into something larger.

In the painting the malleability of spatial ideas becomes more and more vivid as we see the Bank of England large in one place and small in another, as we follow bridges across the figured carpet and finally notice the little figure who is drawing at a table in the foreground, dwarfed by the models, most of which are several times his height. Is he a model too, just the right doll to live in the doll's houses of this papery city, contained in a room?

Soane didn't just hypothesize about models, he collected them, forming a conglomerate not unlike Gandy's picture. He had stands built on which to display them, including the tiered set now in the center of the model room, which in Soane's time usurped prime space in his sitting room, so taken was he with a large cork model of the excavations at Pompeii. This not only gave Gandy the idea for his cutaway view of the Bank of England (the so called Bank in Ruins) but probably contributed to Soane's lantern and dome effects, which are architecture dissected, in which walls become semitransparent or figmental. Both models and Soane's own architectural imagination make conceptual experience primary.

Thus what seems confusing, even senseless to some observers, Rome and Paestum jostling each other as if they are in the same place, is just the effect Soane seeks. Models free us from literal constraints to make impossible comparisons with ease. Soane's models invite imaginary perambulations in which the eye is overwhelmed by one thing, then another, creating a phantasmagoric experience: the spatial art, which requires travel, has been internalized. But his interest in models as serious playthings is something it would be hard to get any current practitioner to admit to.

Piling model on model this way gives one's sense of place and scale a jarring shake like a mental earthquake, exacerbating a potential dormant in all models, to make distance unreal and thus free us from our own spatial identity. Even bird's-eye views like du Cerceau's series of French chateaux let you "walk round" them like models, getting a visual grasp of a complex group without changing your position. In du Cerceau there is no room for the trivia of existence, only empty courtyards and gardens like printed patterns: for him architecture is enough. Unlike most models, du Cerceau's buildings are weightless solids, insubstantial pure idea; thus he avoids shading in suggesting volume. The great beauty of these buildings, apart from their watchlike intricacy, is that they appear to be made largely of air.

On the rare occasions when one experiences a natural bird's-eye view, one realizes just how many idealizing conventions have been applied in pictures or models which take this vantage point. Český Krumlov in south Bohemia has a well-deserved reputation as an unusually intact old town. The core fills a pendulous bulge in the course of a river. Opposite and high above stands the castle, from which the town appears a compact mass as if heaped on a plate whose edge is the river. This bird's-eye view offers a number of things no model can, yet it also reveals certain deficiencies. Our view is often interrupted and we are left guessing, for example, how a building continues when something comes in front of it. In fact, comprehending how the parts fit together needs working out. Revealing the plan is not a high priority, nor have parts been colored to make things easier. One can see that a few simple devices would clarify this.

If only one could apply a little light shading so that one knew the canyon of a street lay between certain sets of buildings. Most of all, any contrived view or miniature replica reduces the confusing interference of forms with each other. Perhaps at times planners' influence has extended so far that restrictions have been formulated purely with a view to clarifying the bird's-eye aspect of the place. Certainly with relatively inexpensive changes of coloring and materials one could bring about a more intelligible picture. The question is whether and how often, outside Disneyland, this technique of turning real places into models has actually been practiced.

The entertainment staged for Queen Elizabeth's visit to Elvetham in 1591 turned a whole landscape into a model. This is now mainly known from a contemporary engraving which shows a crescent-shaped island in a crescent-shaped lake in which swim a sea god, a troop of naiads, miniature warships, and other paraphernalia of sea battles. The scenery celebrates Elizabeth as the ruler of the seas who is virgin like the goddess Diana, represented by her emblem a crescent moon, which controls the tides. The Queen's claim to semidivine status rested in important part on her virginity and wasn't damaged by repeated unsuccessful marriage negotiations on her behalf.

The print shows things from above or silhouetted in the same view, whichever is convenient. Thus we have a grasp of the layout which remained beyond the original spectators, who are presented like the counters on a game board, all distinct and non-overlapping. The landscape is dotted with compact buildings, miniature in relation to the figures and grotesquely large vis-a-vis lake, banks, and islands. Shrinkage and expansion of natural proportions are introduced willfully in the service of meaning. In the resulting environment our own scale suddenly seems very large, as if we had wandered onto a children's playground.

In Japanese gardens such bird's-eye views are often actually built. The main garden at Sambo-in in Kyoto contains episodes at an extremely different scale from their surroundings. These can be read as model landscapes where clipped shrubs stand for boulders, large trees, or whole forests. Here you lose track of scale immersing yourself in a corner where the world becomes as it were more concentrated. But then you will wake up, catching sight of a large tree that arches over the entire miniature landscape.

Perhaps the greatest juggler of scales and creator of conceptual spaces in Western art is Pieter Bruegel. The most model-like treatment of the issues, balanced between centralizing and centrifugal forces, is his Tower of Babel in Vienna. Here is an attempt to present all human culture and intellectual effort as a single enterprise, as one great building under an expansive sky.

The grasp and subordination of detail is astonishing but intimates defeat: human wills are hopelessly diverse and go on getting further away from each other while adjacent. Bruegel's own curiosity is a lonely phenomenon, and the paintings throw us back on ironic perception (how little anyone realizes the staring distances between them) as a substitute for human cohesion.

Bruegel still has a foot in a world which imagines geometric perfection to be the natural state of things, but all his separate observations tend to undermine any alignment between human culture and the physical universe. The earlier idealism can be seen at full strength in a little miniature of the Hill of Knowledge by a fifteenth-century follower of Botticelli. Here a model isn't just the pattern for a single pleasing structure but an intimation of cosmic law. The picture shows a precipitous hill around which a spiral path winds, on which seven stages are marked. These are the seven Liberal Arts in their conventional order from Grammar at the bottom to Theology at the top, each represented by two figures: a female personification and a famous historical exemplar, male. The hierarchy of human intellectual activity fits a divine plan, so that the structure of a medieval university translates easily into a geographical feature.

The centralized buildings which transfixed so many Renaissance architects were little models of the universe. It is hard to imagine Bramante playing as lightheartedly with the idea as Pietro da Cortona does in a proposal for a miniature building made of six small domed temples stacked 3-2-1 to form a rich architectural cake or mountain, like six universes or a whole aspiring city of door and window frames.

This conceit, which looks as much like an altar tabernacle as a garden pavilion, is just a bit of flattery for a papal patron. Among Alexander VII Chigi's family emblems is a device familiar from Borromini's S. Ivo, six hills or miniature mountains clumped in stylized, pyramidal form. The image condensed this way has been reexpanded and recivilized by Cortona. If you remember the emblem, the pavilion is ludicrously huge and elaborate. If you think of the mountains, it seems extremely precious. Which sensation predominates—inflation or belittling? In either case frivolity rules.

At Gonville and Caius College, Cambridge, a learned amateur uses an architectural compendium to express a soberer purpose. The sixteenth-century refounder of this college created a little allegorical journey across the quadrangle, marking the stages of students' progress with pieces of architecture. The last point on this journey, which had previously passed through Gates of Humility and Virtue, was the Gate of Honour.

This structure combines a number of partly incompatible ideas: first a three-bay arch with wide central opening. Then, perched atop it and squeezed so the whole temple fits over the opening, a highly decorated cube with pediments on all four sides and porticos back and front. On top of this, a dome or lantern on a high octagonal base. The temple is very condensed; the cupola which crowns it seems correspondingly stretched or expanded and sits within a fence of spindly finials. The overall effect is both dignified and awkward, tapering and almost spirelike. Perhaps its pronounced oddity makes it more plausible as the bearer of weighty meanings which it places upon you as you cross the threshold. It exemplifies the model as a vehicle of moral import.

Another small building hoisted out of reach, which therefore seems loaded with unattainable significance, sits atop the tower of Hawksmoor's St. George Bloomsbury. It's a many-stepped pyramid, a classical tomb form oddly met in a Christian context and resembling a spire only remotely, but intimating by its untoward placing and model-like reduction an insoluble intellectual mystery.

The great archetype of small symbolic structures, Bramante's Tempietto at S. Pietro in Montorio, Rome, has a clearer program than Hawksmoor's. This little centralized temple marks the traditional site of St. Peter's crucifixion, so it is a shrine commemorating a painful martyrdom. But it doesn't seem to make specific reference to the death. There are no agonies in its form, quite the contrary. It is quintessentially harmonious, and if it sat in the intended circular courtyard, whose colonnade would echo the Tempietto's, the effect would be stronger still. Externally the only signs of Peter's ordeal are decorous emblems in the metopes of the frieze which one needs to come very near to recognize.

It is tempting to see Bramante's building as a purely architectural utterance. He has reduced the scale of the ideal form, a circular space crowned by a dome and ringed by a colonnade, to the point where a door frame adequate to the human frame won't quite fit within adjacent pilasters in the wall. So the building verges on being too small for feasibility or at least enterability. It is an interesting problem for an ambitious architect, to build the smallest possible building of such perfect form, which gives the satisfaction models give, of being grasped so comfortably by the mind.

The Tempietto commemorates St. Peter's death, supposed to have happened here. Attempts were often made to transport an important event to another place by erecting a model of a structure associated with it. In medieval England the Lady Richelde saw Christ's childhood home in a dream and was instructed by her vision to have a replica built in Walsingham, a relatively obscure spot in Norfolk but nearer for English pilgrims than the original Nazareth. Giovanni Rucellai brought back measurements of Christ's sepulchre from the Holy Land intending to have the space which Christ had vacated, the empty shell of the miracle, reproduced in Florence. In the end Alberti, his architect, didn't follow the measurements exactly, opting for a more fanciful or perfect construction. His replica is a building within a building, neatly set off by marble paving in the center of a high vaulted space. Though very small, this little shrine is apsed and capped with a tall fringe like a crown of leaves. Its walls are incongruously beautified with Christian symbols and Rucellai insignia alternating in marble inlay, two-dimensional, nonarchitectural, a kind of embroidery more retrograde than the exquisite Corinthian pilasters and frieze which organize the papery walls of this construction whose stylish inscription reveals a collision of worldly and spiritual purposes.

An even more remarkable sequence brought Mary's childhood home to Loreto on the Adriatic coast. This little building flew through the air, steered by angels and making an intermediate stop near Fiume. When it finally settled and a town grew up around it, it was itself encased in a rich scenic coating of discordantly luxurious character, which reduces it to the status of a miniature, no longer big enough for the scale of the cult it has inspired.

Instead of bringing Nazareth to London, Wren planned a centralized domed church. His so-called Great Model for St. Paul's, the realest form the idea ever got, is now displayed in the crypt of the building he actually built and remains one of the most persuasive advocates of the centralized domed church, which it shows can have great power without great dimensions. It might reasonably become a shrine to which admirers of this architect would have to repair to gauge his full stature.

The theory of such a design is that you don't need Nazareth in London, because the physical force of this grand geometrical idea creates a spiritual focus here. It initiates you into the laws of the cosmos and of matter, reinstituted rather than replicated in the model, which is so powerful because it is the model of a model.

Models and model-like procedures often function as revealers or dissectors of reality, showing things the building never could which therefore remain buried within it. There is a model of the extraordinary home Melnikov built for himself in the increasingly hostile political climate of Moscow in 1927, which swivels open to reveal its secrets like a doll's house. This house consists of two large interlocking cylinders, and the model makes Melnikov's point about the overlapping of these two forms extremely clearly. It also lets us imagine the various ways we would perceive one of these cylinders from the other, and the way we would *fail* to perceive the relation at certain points because an interior wall separated us by inches from the other volume.

Sometimes features remain invisible not because they are hard to demonstrate properly, but because the architect wants it that way. The parapets which disguise the true external volume of St. Paul's, adding a story to the aisles which isn't really there, can be seen but not appreciated as fakery from the ground. A model or a cutaway drawing (rather than a plain section) is the most effective way to make the deception visible.

In certain Baroque designs harmonies between external contour and plan come out better in drawings than in reality, and best of all in a model form like isometric rendering seen from beneath with the floor removed. This is not a technique Borromini himself used, but it seems ideal for showing the relation between internal volumes, external forms, and certain features of the plan in Sette Dolori for example.

Borromini is an interesting case because crucial features of his designs, like the geometric skeleton for S. Ivo say, are difficult to experience in the building. One's only hope would seem to be working up from diagrams to models, but some will feel that they are only being led further and further astray in being asked to study features of buildings which can't be perceived by the senses on the spot.

Buildings themselves sometimes replicate the sensation of seeing the same thing twice which you get from drawings that splice a section and a plan, bringing part of the second in collision with the first as if these modes could be simultaneous. Guarini's little church projects are presented this way in his *Architettura civile*, while his most complex designs, the two lantern domes in Turin, are like plans exploding upward but always retaining a quasi-graphic intricacy as their primary quality.

The spectator investigates these spaces in a peculiar way, not by sailing unthinking into them but by working out how one might get there—by generating them intellectually, however haltingly. But then a high intricate vault or dome often challenges the user to a strenuous exercise. It is as if our normal coordinates have been violated by rotating the world ninety degrees. As if one were to enter a theater and find the stage receding into the roof, the actors all defying gravity with no difficulty, and our seats on the ground as usual. Illusions painted, carved, or built on or into the ceiling don't start from easy acceptance of human bodily form and capacities. One is inclined to say that by contrast a proscenium stage makes things very easy, presenting an enterable model of the world of comfortably restricted dimensions. But one is always held at bay, not just when too far from the front or interfered with by a post. Two frustrations impede us: there isn't all that much of the perfect simulated world, and one must remain content with viewing it from afar. Two or three members of the audience wandering through the set would not utterly destroy the illusion: it couldn't accommodate them all.

Stage sets are a whole class of enterable model (though most of us are not allowed entry) which supply the pattern for certain kinds of architecture like the shop interiors of Nigel Coates. The false perspectives on the stage at the Teatro Olimpico are covered in false people (statues on cornices and in niches) who compete with the real ones playing false parts. This is one of those places where the urge is strongest to test the perspectives and see what the geometry of the deception is, perhaps because it has real architectural ambitions and perhaps even something to teach about grand vistas in full-size cities.

Nearly akin to the proscenium stage is a whole class of model very suggestive for strictly architectural members of the genre. This is the diorama, a little world whose dimensions may be a sort of life size, as with small natural history specimens, though this may only mean a patch of mountain habitat the size of a large closet. Or, most engaging of all, a whole Indian tribe's ways within a frame three feet by two. This is by no means the limit of smallness. Perhaps to get the most from the idea one should carefully traverse the whole gamut of sizes. Dolls survive from almost every known culture, though in some the line is hard to draw between the paraphernalia of momentous ritual and the toys of children, but then to the young play is often magic ritual.

In a Portuguese church under a large painting of a suffering saint is a little cavity framed in gold and fronted with glass like a little reliquary cabinet. Inside it we find not the powdery bones we expect, with their papery authentication attached, but a fully equipped doll's room thoughtfully lit by a little desk lamp projected on a shelf in front of it.

Presiding within is a doll six inches tall in rich ecclesiastical garb seated at a rococo desk with quill pen poised in midair. On the desk are a wealth of supplies including the bishop's miter he has taken off and the skull which pulls his thoughts back to final things. Behind him a wall of books, around him a surprising collection of pitchers and jars for watering spiritual gardens, empty chairs for visitors who never come, and best of all a diminutive glass shrine, from which a saint even smaller than he looks out. Dolls must have their dolls, their pets, their concentrated versions.

So what are the uses of the little saint? The Protestant view of Southern religion has seen it as grownups taken in by frippery and playing with dolls, as if high spiritual meaning could be carried by the stuffs sold in a haberdasher's. But the scale makes all the difference and this little person inspires a more innocent form of awe. Perhaps one can imagine a continuum leading from the doll to the standing Christ or the mummified saint in its glass coffin under the retable. Perhaps there is a quotient of play as there certainly is of imaginative reconstruction in the meditation on any image, which is always an incomplete representation of the event to be contemplated.

Part of the magic in very condensed images may be brought out best by the ultimate in framing, the dense manuscript pages fashioned by Giulio Clovio near the end of that tradition. Almost anyone will recognize that Clovio's model is the most gigantic of all painted surfaces, the Sistine ceiling. So the most exquisite takes its cue from the most impossibly vast. Michelangelo consumed less than four years covering the Sistine ceiling; Clovio spent nine focusing onto his tiny surfaces that huge crowd of writhing figures.

It is a commonplace that much of Michelangelo's energy has migrated to the borders and to the sometimes nameless figures who stand guard on or lift like heavy weights the scenes from biblical narrative.

Clovio takes this further. The border population has got even more numerous and various. They are shown as cast in bronze and gilded, or as carved from ivory or other exquisite substances, but they possess more vivid life than the little painted actors toward whom they strain. Here is an extreme instance of toys taking over the life of their owner and the center of our attention further and further displaced until it hardly makes sense anymore to ask where reality lies.

Of this particular act of obsessive depiction perhaps the goal is a thorough loss of self, dispersed into minutiae which offer smaller and smaller lenses for looking in on a universe which shrinks obligingly to smaller and smaller dimensions. In a more normative instance of the diorama, Antonello della Messina's *St. Jerome in His Study,* the idea is more prosaic and suggests among other things that a model is a kind of storage. The saint inhabits a room within a room within a room, which is further divided into a set of drawers and cupboards, some full, some empty, it doesn't matter. The key is to set us going on the path that Noah followed, collecting things and bringing them back to our ark where they make sense simply by being there. Reality can be saved by packing it away, but we prefer to leave the fronts off the drawers and the doors off the cupboards, to save us the futility of getting our equipment out again only to put it back and so on.

Sometimes we meet pieces of furniture masquerading as whole buildings which intimate a world of reduced dimensions, like living in a diorama. Robert Smythson's chimneypieces in the Little Castle at Bolsover (its name an understatement) are themselves castles, with story piled on story. Smythson is building the world all over again on a smaller scale. More ambitious or preposterous attempts have popped up in twentieth-century America. Disneyland is probably an idea which grew and grew, adding on bits from far-flung sources. It soon picked up protective educational coloring, but what havoc would it not wreak with its learners' view of reality, putting Gothic castles at the foot of the Matterhorn, next to alligator-infested swamps? The key to Disneyland is that everything is about five-eighths its normal size, big enough to pass itself off on adults who've come to play with dolls.

In Colonial Williamsburg it is generally considered an enhancement of historical reality that in the kitchens women make candles and in the forge a smith is shoeing horses. They are not just doing it but explaining as they go, models which talk, in a world which relentlessly depicts itself to us. Everything is in its natural location, kitchen gardens, fences, unpaved roads, even taverns which feed us with authentic food and antiquated intoxicants, but everything is an exhibit too. Though the stage is not a grand one, the play gives meaning to every moment.

In the models of Hitler's New Berlin the scale is larger. The giveaway in the case of these ministries with their endless facades is the tiny people and cars which speckle the ground in front of them. Can we posit a cynical architect who adjusted the grandeur of his scheme by trying out tinier and tinier figures in the foreground? Hitler took a fanatical interest in these models—did he know this was the only form his New Berlin would ever take? There are photographs which show him peering down the Lilliputian boulevards: so much for the innocence of play. Delusions of grandeur are a risk models run: believing them too well, we turn their experiments with sizes into serious errors of scale and then really feel like rulers.

Sometimes size isn't an issue. Buildings actually built can remind us of models not by their smallness but by looking like a kit of parts and therefore a kind of demonstration left incomplete on purpose. Certain Coop Himmelblau projects are most radical of this kind. It comes as a surprise to learn that models play a large part in their genesis from the earliest stages. Not quite the earliest of all—as we suspected, an irresponsible drawing is the starting point, but then a long defining process begins which bounces ping-pong-like between model and drawing, becoming continually more precise.

The outcome, in something like the rooftop lawyers' offices in Vienna, hardly looks as if it could be built, and at the same time reveals its structure or its buildedness with unheard-of frankness. If it makes spectators uncomfortable it must be because they see *too much* of how it is made. Maybe it is easier to imagine how it would fall apart than how it will stay up.

Here the translation is fascinating, but this is still an object translated from another medium into architecture. The model and the building are both realizations of the drawing, which possesses a certain quotient of unlikelihood that they have lost. We would like to find a model more impossible than any drawing, and Frank Gehry's Familian house may be a candidate. It flouts every conceivable idea of a finished object. It is like a walk which consists entirely of falling down, repeatedly making forward progress only because it stumbles in a consistent direction. It plays with the ability of models to explain, suggesting that the comprehensible world they always conjure up is just a beguiling fiction.

6
Ideas

How does one recognize an idea, in reality and then in architecture? An idea is a kind of ordering or pattern-making which can be appreciated most easily in architecture through extreme and concentrated instances where the concept is not recessive, taking its place quietly, but obtrusive. Some would call such foreign implants, not fully digested into architecture, conceits. Many of them still smack of the other modes from which they partly derive, mathematical, literary, or philosophical.

There is a class of architects who regard themselves as thinkers, who produce treatises and view the art as a mentally strenuous and testing activity. Their productions are habitually difficult and present problems of understanding.

Ledoux is one of them, for whom buildings often take the form of almost perfect mathematical or geometrical figures. In his ideal community at Chaux he projected distinctive dwellings for many sorts of worker, including the hoopmaker who made the iron bands which bound the wooden wheels of all vehicles. Ledoux's design for the hoopmaker's house depicts this band enlarged and projected through the depth of a few rooms. Merged with this circle with a gaping hole in it is a duplicate placed at right angles to it. In elevation the result is a circle inscribed in a square, an even more perforated-feeling form.

The further it is carried the more anti-practical this conception seems, and it provokes the question of what the abstract pattern means. What is the point of the fiercely held geometrical proposition? In Ledoux's houses for operatives the key seems to be a notion of political or mental control. Lives are subordinated to architectural concepts as if they barely existed.

The house for a river supervisor presents us with the same configuration which now has water running through it, one of the strangest of all invasions of human building by an external force. At Wright's Fallingwater, which might appear to offer a parallel balance of forces, the meaning of the water is utterly different and the flow less strictly regulated. Ledoux's version makes the dwelling a kind of echo chamber and converts the natural element to an inescapable din.

Many people must have looked at the familiar image of this project without grasping the intended scale. You think of it as a section of sewer pipe until you notice the little mill buildings in the foreground. In fact Ledoux conceives his exercise in solids and voids on a monumental scale. One of the most significant features of his work is the way similar forms turn up in many different sizes. The gatehouse at Chaux repeats this same spouting cylinder or donut, demurely reduced to a dripping urn. Here the flow is arrested, carved in stone to represent winter or eternity. The effect is something like rustication, a wild natural energy depicted statically like a standoff between cold thoughts and hot feelings.

The most grandiose occurrence of this favored form, the perfect circle with a hole in it, is the public space at the center of the community at Chaux. This enormous donut contains the industrial heart of the settlement along with the director's house and barracks for workers. On this vaster scale both the geometrical figure and the emptiness are more intensely loaded: Ledoux's universe is a place where an authoritarian schema is elicited by an overpowering sense of the void which surrounds it and which it also pretends to enclose in symbolic form.

A different route and a different goal led Louis Kahn to similar forms. The main building of the National Assembly at Dacca has the circle inscribed in the square at its heart. In plan this may look like a strong form trapped or held prisoner in a weaker one: experientially the cylindrical core is something like a void and the most interesting and problematic spaces are the interstices between the two fused geometries, internal streets which are neither one nor the other and form a buffer zone like a Middle Eastern market between administrative and ceremonial spaces. The edges of these spaces are defined by walls pierced by huge circular openings across which run the slanting lines of ramps. As in Ledoux, the emptiness and shadow surrounding these indications of routes signify profound thought which has plumbed dark depths.

Across the malarial lake, in which Kahn insisted on isolating the legislature like a medieval plague hospital inside its moat, are some jollier structures—hostels for officials in warm brick, a less thoroughly alien material in this exotic setting than the concrete and marble which Kahn specified for the main building.

In the hostels, exuberant play with elementary geometry— perfect cubes and squat cylinders boldly punctured by circles and half moons—reminds us of Ledoux's building blocks, which supply different dwellings for a dozen classes of worker. Such play is more like the manipulation of a stock of archetypes than that anguished search for the lost roots of architecture and the deepest meaning of the activities he is trying to give a home to, which is Kahn's way of depicting his own creative process.

In the library for Exeter Academy in New Hampshire Kahn reverts to an eighteenth-century type, the library as an emblematic representation of all knowledge. Here the circle is inscribed in the square on the internal elevations only: the library is a hermetic building type. For once the figure's meaning is clear: knowledge is collected in one spot, is then focused and ignites. The experience of users is in some sense communal: they view all the books at once, a sensation which transcends the encounter with any one of them. Such meanings dominate Kahn's work, and luckily for him most of his later clients were educational or cultural institutions which had the time and patience to indulge in the philosophical discourse which Kahn came to think architecture was.

Radical geometrical experiments of slightly later date are more likely to be private and noncommunal, even noncommunicative, like John Hejduk's Bye Residence of 1972–1974. This embodies an outrageous reaction to the idea of the building as a clear geometrical figure. It has shrunk to a dimensionless wall which is being inspected by work crews or intruders in the form of rooms which attach themselves momentarily at intervals along its length. Habitation is literally extraneous to the main enterprise.

Hejduk's explorations of the theme (whose alienated character is expressed by numbering the projects as the only way of keeping them straight) are maniacally persistent, proving that impossibility is an objective, not a by-product. The building becomes an anti-figure or no-figure, a set of deeply disconnected episodes for the contemplation of a wall.

The attack on the whole idea of dimension and real space in architecture which we sense here has its true fulfillment on paper. This project embodies an anti-architectural *concept* which would inevitably lose some of its force if we tried to turn it into architecture, for the purest and most severe concepts cannot enter reality without loss. When architecture is thinking itself out of existence we would do it no favor by offering it the chance to build its cancellation on a certain street in a particular suburb.

Hejduk's houses are socially if not technically impossible to build because they so violate what any conceivable user would want in a house. In fact their main aim is to thwart integration in any imaginable life, and their force comes from making you think about that anti-life, but they don't really advise you to try it. So if one was built—and maybe this would be a way of taking the thinking more seriously—it would be the model of an idea, and not a house.

Hejduk's houses are rarefied examples of architecture as pure geometrical inquiry. More accessible instances occur in Czech Cubism. Here too architecture was conceived as having a geometric identity prior to and stronger than its function. In a modest villa like one of Janak's in Pelhřimov of 1912–1913, comparison with its neighbor which abuts shows the elements to be versions of dormer, window frame, and porch post, not the pure sculpture they pretend to be. A frequent criticism of these so-called Cubist buildings, whose link with Picasso is tenuous, is that the radicalism is only skin deep. But leaving aside questions of how the forms are actually constructed, they suggest an underlying solid mass from which a house is carved. This, we are meant to believe, is a special crystalline substance, not a conventionally put together building. The trouble is that these radical ideas about the nature of the object are conveyed in tricks of rendering which may depend at certain points on wooden framing or special brickwork but are essentially efforts of the plasterer. So although the ideas are not superficial, the execution is. Finally, even at this level the deviations from normality are rather tame: the clustered crystals of the porch props are the same each time, and thus obedient to a system from outside the world of crystals.

The other architectural work with a claim to be considered Cubist includes a very special venture into design by a philosopher who probed the logical structures underlying many cultural expressions. In 1926 Ludwig Wittgenstein designed a house for his sister in Vienna. It is impossible to examine it without looking for an embodiment of Wittgenstein's ideas about the nature of the universe or at least of cultural forms in general, but we might find after all that he has simply fit himself to a specialized mode, architecture, with a result which has little bearing outside a narrow precinct. In fact Wittgenstein's design breeds some disappointment of this sort: his house is more like other houses than his thinking is like other thought.

It is ghostly architecture with evasive refinements like vestigial beams and slightly receding capitals—pure and noncommittal at the same time. The hall with its glass doors is one of the most characteristic spaces, like a picture of a kind of thought which has lots of structure and little content. One can detect here his interest in the rules of games almost in isolation from the experience of playing them. It is a mind more interested in principles than details, which feels the main lines would be obscured if you filled them in.

Externally nothing is stated which can't be verified. Extraordinarily few liberties are taken, yet all this searching honesty leads to a slightly nondescript result. The most striking feature is perhaps the thick platform the house sits on, as if to stake it out as a mental location in a frankly constructed, not naturally occurring universe.

Wittgenstein's contemporary and mentor Adolf Loos is one of the most perplexing designers in the same mode. In late works like the Müller house in Prague internal spaces and forms interlock like objects in a Cubist painting. The seating alcove of a woman's dressing room looks out through a grille onto the stepped composition of sitting room leading onto dining room. The process of thought rises through increments to an appreciation of the solidity of space itself. So it is as if the house is full of a palpable presence before you inhabit it, or as if it contained mineral oil not air. The aim of interconnected spaces in Loos is an intellectual contemplation of the nature of space; he doesn't provide usable rooms but volumes which are probably not very adaptable.

Loos's formal vocabulary looks deceptively neutral, consisting of variations on rectangular solids. Member of an Italian group called Rationalists, Giuseppe Terragni's best work is even more fiercely intellectual than Loos's and doesn't allow itself the sybaritic materials and textures we are surprised to find in Loos interiors. Once again the pure geometry is baffling—clear like an equation, but what is it trying to say? In a carefully formulated work like the Casa del Fascio (now Popolo) in Como, his home town, Terragni comes as near to a contentless statement, a pure empty thought pattern, as anyone ever has.

Terragni is fascinated by voids, which are given a more powerful presence than the adjacent solids. Perhaps it is the sophisticated blotting out of thought, a procedure which would have its use under Fascist rule.

Such surgery is more radical still in the Casa Rustici, a block of flats designed in 1936–1937 for Milan. This is a building which wishes away much of its substance, as if it would like to claim nonexistence. After carving and excision have had their way we are left with stringy tissue, a skeleton rather than a fleshed-out body. From its internal court the building's integrity seems even more hypothetical: it feels like two adjacent, fairly proximate blocks which in pulling further apart have stretched the slender links between them, catwalks and balconies different in character from the Russian Constructivist features which may form part of their inspiration. This is no expression of social dynamism but represents the tentative quality of thought, putting something forward which you may decide to retract.

A recent self-declared admirer of Terragni, Peter Eisenman, sees him as a passionless manipulator. This is the striking and liberating feature of Eisenman's own designs, who has had an important influence on students through his licensing of arbitrary experimentation. House III of 1969–1970 consists of a cube within a cube, the one rotated forty-five degrees against the other. The strength of the idea is its complete neglect of use and all other social reality. It has jumped from paper into the world without softening or adaptive modification.

Larger projects like *Moving Arrows* of 1985 make a similar thought process even clearer. Here an arbitrary geometry is planted or overlaid on a whole existing settlement (the clash which was internal to House III), and arbitrariness itself is thus more starkly revealed as the determining feature of thought. By that means human design declares its freedom to choose or invent. In Terragni the void of meaning finds some of its explanation in an oppressive regime. In Eisenman no such constraints are declared. "Because I want it like that" is never a complete explanation, however. To the extent that Eisenman's designs are authentic expressions of something, they mark out a spiritual void, and they appeal to us not through their cleverness or mastery but through their abject admission of the collapse of meaning.

Cleverness is not unknown as a disguise for deep cultural disquiets. Mannerism has been seen as such a mechanism, staving off painful realizations by means of mental tangles which it challenges you to untie. A rood screen of 1533–1534 in Limoges cathedral presents a clear instance—freestanding indoor architecture of mind-boggling complexity. At either end of this stone construction, now moved to the west end of the nave, is a spiral staircase on which are depicted two competing classical systems, a horizontal one carried over from the body of the screen, a spiral or diagonal one which follows the rising line of steps curving round a central post like a rolled newspaper.

There are intense moments of collision where moldings overlap or intersect, and sensations of squashing and stretching where the elongated diagonal sets off from or comes to rest against sober flatness. The result may not be truly classical, but it is certainly productive of thought. Strange intersections bred by two systems conjoined work like axonometric representation to show you more sides than are usually visible. All the elements, normative or distorted, are dislodged from their rightful places and brought to life.

There are of course projects which seek out conflict even more aggressively than the stair at Limoges. Federico Zuccaro's very original facade for his house in Florence derives refined intellectual stimulus from harsh junctures between smooth and rough stonework. Elements of the facade have a ravaged look like half-destroyed remnants left on a battlefield, but they are set in an ashlar background which makes all the difference; someone is using contradiction to generate energy. This facade is like a discussion between opponents, one of whom is always in danger of being marginalized. Windows are thrust or crowded to the edge; preserving them is not a high priority; it feels as if they may disappear. Somehow, and not just through the narrowness of the space, the composition makes us think we may fall off the edge too.

There are those who hold out for more literal interpretations of Mannerist works. To them the discords of this facade are simply multiplied artifice, not a plumbing of subjective depths, and strapwork is really superfice, not an investigation of mental tangles and impediments, a sort of churning of the mind which keeps returning you to the same place. Of course an unimaginative producer can pick up the tics of a style and repeat them not comprehending the potential for meaningful expression. This undoubtedly is what strapwork becomes in some hands, idle tying and untying of knots which fill space the way games of patience fill time. But any mode can be practiced either trivially or profoundly, and there are enough anguished examples of the form to convince us that the idle version is not its true fulfillment.

In certain works the ambiguities are so startling that literal interpretations aren't possible. Buontalenti's stairs to the choir of S. Stefano in Florence are like cartilaginous tissue in stone and must cause the most prosaic foot to hesitate before planting itself on this unfolded fan of living substance. Our unease springs partly from the incongruity: a monster's gullet or ear flap this near the altar? Most things resemble other things hereabout: balusters are like funeral urns or at least elegant vases which probably secrete a thick liquid. Metamorphic shifts are the norm here and apparently nothing has a straightforward identity.

The painter Arcimboldo specializes in such presentations in the famous series of human busts made of other things. The person becomes a building constructed of consistent but totally unsuitable components. Thus his allegory of *Fire* shows a man made of things *on* fire, things forged or cast *(using* fire), and things designed to *hold* fire or to *be set on* fire (lamps, candles, and explosives). The ideal viewer takes pleasure in misuse and distortion, won't learn much—for the view of reality is highly conventional—and needs to enjoy complication for its own sake. And he or she must also countenance the deliberate cultivation of an alienated perspective. For modern users Arcimboldo's images are momentary hallucinations shut up in books. In their initial form they were paintings which didn't disappear once you had got the joke or worked out most of the resemblances.

Likewise the harpies at the four corners of Giambologna's Neptune fountain in Bologna were not passing phantoms but permanent concretions of uncomfortable splits. They come very near in fact to being ideal personifications of the slippery contradictions present in nonfigurative Mannerist architecture and design, being both lewd and cold, elegant and slimy. They represent a sensuality which is oppressively vivid yet alien as well, which one feels pulled toward and repelled from at the same time, suggesting that much of the power of Mannerist works comes from bringing into the open a discomfort over sexual desire.

A sensation of discomfort is also central to much of Borromini's work. Muffled passion breaks out in odd unions between discordant forms: a concave facade is topped by a convex mass which starts out looking like the drum of a dome and turns into an archaeological fairy tale. This is his design for the university church of S. Ivo in Rome where he could presumably afford a sprinkling of learned references. The crowning feature is a lantern in spiral form which represents a heavenly ascent by the intellect.

Another ascent, like Borromini turned inside out, occurs in the chapel Guarini made to hold the Holy Shroud in Turin. The shroud is a ghostly apparition of Christ's physical form which is said to have been transferred to the cloth which wrapped his corpse. Guarini's idea of an appropriate housing for this figment is an architectural apparition mostly suspended beyond our physical reach like a spiritual temptation. It is another mathematician's riddle with supernatural implications.

Looking up into the dome one finds a system like a focusing lens or a teetering stick construction made of an inconceivable number of distinct parts. The infusion of the supernatural comes in the separate introduction of light into the space at every stage of the ascent. In fact every one of the piled-up arches which constitute this climbing feature, imitating in sophisticated form the most primitive method of constructing something tall, is subdivided and admits two slabs of light.

Guarini employs far less imagery than Borromini, yet with considerable overlap in the symbolism; stars, rays of light, and sunbursts are depicted in both. Guarini concentrates more singly on the mysteries and potentialities of light, the medium by which the image was impressed on the shroud and the form in which the architect prefers to depict the Being who ordains earthly miracles.

The most powerful experience of these finally ungraspable realities comes through intellectual contemplation of the mystery held away from us at a distance, not in anything too easy or readily available to the senses. Difficulty remains an essential element of the highest truths, and Guarini's greatest achievement as an architect is a subjective intensification of this perception.

The eighteenth-century Bohemian architect Giovanni Santini (whose family had emigrated from Italy two or three generations earlier) practices distortions which approach the grotesque. But they are the distortions of a mathematician, produced by the bowing and gnarling of standard figures. An intricate cemetery chapel he built near Zdar is his S. Ivo in its concentrated extravagance, like a little intellectual crystal. It lies inside complex outworks: a polygonal figure set in a larger one (the perimeter wall) whose sides alternate between concavity and convexity, broken in the middle by six pavilions, momentary bulges in the general hollowing. Their windows are triangles losing their shape through a bloating pressure which forces their sides out. The result is a form vaguely Gothic but beginning to disintegrate. Stuck down on top of it is a decidedly eighteenth-century hipped roof whose angles are played off against its curves. Santini delights in multiple perspectives and his forms feel reversible: the wall or the window is concave or convex depending on whether you regard it from inside or outside.

The larger central chapel is one of the most bowed, distorted constructions ever, some of whose bowed forms are Gothic: windows have pointed arches, proportions of main elements are spindly or slender, but Gothic means here a tortured and converging geometry hijacked (as by Feininger) for expressive purposes.

And Gothic windows are contained within swooping Baroque gables whose slopes are perhaps a bit steeper than any straight Baroque, thus suggesting teetery and undependable psychic states. Santini is at home in a topsy-turvy world where the Gothic arch is a vector driving toward a lopsided consummation and where ultraregular starting points lead to something misshapen.

To what kind of faith does it correspond? A religion full of riddles and inconsistencies, in which you come at the truth in quantum leaps, not by steady progress. It is an uneven reality where the main use of rational calculation is to undermine reason.

Santini's relation to history is original and disconcerting. At Zdar Gothic forms become fair game deprived of their familiar context. Elsewhere he commandeers Renaissance allegory and applies it to vulgar uses. At Ostrov nad Oslavou Santini built a hostelry in the form of a giant letter W. There must have been a reference to the proprietor or landowner which is now lost, leaving pure meaningless symbol. But from the beginning there was a contrast between the abstract idea and the muddled and uneven reality. The strengths of different legs of the letter are wildly disparate, the central core two stories, the outer wings only one. The figure has less than nothing to do with the building's function or even with any conceivable idea of writing or language.

But then what was ever meant by buildings in the shape of conventional figures—stars, letters, or personal insignias? Not far from Prague the Archduke Ferdinand von Tirol built a hunting lodge two stories high in the form of a six-pointed star. Looking at the plan you feel it is highly inefficient, though the space has been completely carved up in a thoroughly symmetrical way so that each point of the star contains a long diamond-shaped room. Emanating from the center and filling all the remaining space is a system of corridors, many more than convenience requires, each of them ending in a window looking out between two of the star points.

Was it built just to show that it could be done? The points can't have much to do with the compass, which is firmly and unalterably divided in four, nor consequently with practical problems of orientation in the vast hunting preserve by which the lodge is surrounded. We are driven very unsatisfactorily to view it as a mental construct making virtually no reference to anything outside itself. This jewel casket has as many compartments as it has, for no other reason than that it has them.

Idle perfection like this occurs late in the life of a style. Still later phases need to pervert the intentions of classical system still further in order to squeeze enough life from it to keep themselves awake. In these distortions or misuses of the conventional code classicism in architecture becomes a highly intellectual implant, as in the nave windows of Hawksmoor's St. George Bloomsbury which have enormous keystones *under* them, far too big, like thoughts dropped from their proper place and lost. In some technical sense they go with the smaller crypt windows below, which do not have arched tops and therefore don't require keystones. But by now these have become an insignia, marking the center, and have here been intolerably stretched to bridge the gap between the stories, creating a link which is absurd.

Charles Holden's addition to the Law Society of two centuries later is even fuller of elaborate jokes of the same kind, though more decorous in its sense of scale and less ready to assert that stories are not what or where they seem. Keystones have slipped; even windows—the little ones at the corners—have slipped from the frames intended to hold them. Blind forms and nonfunctioning bits predominate. The whole is an almost unpenetrated casket, suggesting the present uselessness of the classical system. Now it is only an object of contemplation, having reverted to pure intellectual construct after years of practical service.

It is an old story, the subversion of classical forms to convey something contrary to their original spirit. In the skyline at Blenheim Vanbrugh and Hawksmoor replicate a medieval fortress, with towers and pinnacles composed of irreproachably classical elements. This is really a more radical project than the mock castle Vanbrugh built for himself, because founded on purposive misreading, like Leonardo finding dragons in water stains and making the hallucination permanent.

Gate piers at Blenheim are hollow jokes worthy of Peter Eisenman, particularly noteworthy for their position on the defensive perimeter (but moved here from a position nearer the house). They are perforated as if by decay, and their strongest elements skewed versus the main mass to become rickety, drafty, and illogical. They form another example of violations of logic as spurs to thought, provoking the spectator to conscious accounting for an untoward form.

In the palace at Blenheim many subversions appear—normally strong elements present themselves as weak, and rational systems are twisted into picturesque silhouettes. Here "Things are not what they seem" is an intellectual challenge, and thinking becomes a process of unraveling the obvious to reach its contrary, the truth. In works by the contemporary American artist Robert Cumming the idea is a riddle which undermines itself and yields two contradictory readings in succession. *Joker on an Angry Sea,* a work in white chalk on black paper which looks like a nineteenth-century wood engraving, shows a lobster boat pitching in heavy seas and forming the upper jaw of a nutcracker face with its own shadow on the wave beneath as the lower jaw. Natural disaster and laboratory experiment—like the party game of casting shadows on the studio wall—are absolutely incompatible.

A similar and more architectural impasse is relished in *Burning Box,* a Cumming work which shows a house-shaped coffer painted all over with heraldic flames in ideal red surrounded by an orange glow more like an actual fire. Again the catastrophe, which would free architecture from stability and allow it to be consumed, is fused with stylized representations of such an event. We conclude that art's relation to activity is bound to be theoretical—it *thinks* about it.

A kind of functional disabling is almost the point of Cumming's art. There are architects or quasi-architectural artists who occupy a similar territory. Daniel Libeskind's *Three Lessons in Architecture* of 1985 are complicated machines which look exceedingly active but substantially pointless. They were actually built, but remain self-driven, self-contained. Their flaps and pulley systems are less impinging and less suggestive of a world outside their own confines than the jittery devices of Jean Tinguely.

Certain drawings by Libeskind stray beyond such narrow limits. The *Micromega* series presents obsessive overlays of many architectural ideas in the same place. Immense fertility is met by disconcerting inability to decide which of the various options to prefer. These works make us wonder if indecision itself might not constitute a mode of thought when recorded scrupulously enough.

From moment to moment in these drawings three-dimensional forms slide through each other and out the other side, all bent on careering journeys, all figments, semitransparent, seen from a vantage point which is like aerial perspective or an axonometric slant. It is a world impossibly *filled*, with forms which are spidery and unstable, a place where everything is supernaturally clear but without center, edge, or hierarchy, where intellectual grasp provides us with our only hold on experience.

Libeskind presents his method of arriving at the form of the Jewish Museum in Berlin as a kind of divination, uncovering a hidden order in congested urban space. Using such foci as Rosa Luxemburg's house, the place where Kafka stayed, Walter Benjamin's family home, and the meridian of Jerusalem, he detects in the layout of the German capital an elongated star of David like a historical shadow cast across the whole city.

When we descend from this scale to the proposed building, tagged onto a stolid existing museum of which Libeskind's jagged addition will be an unnerving alter ego, like the now notional Jewish counterpoint to the dull racial uniformity of Berlin, it isn't obviously taken from this gigantic insignia. Unless it is an intensified fragment of the larger whole, senseless in itself except that it is part of an inscription or diagram the overall meaning of which can only be guessed.

One of the most poignant depictions of the project shows a metallic model of the new structure sitting on a dense page of text. When we look closer this appears to be a list of names like the telephone directory, shorthand for the bewildering multiplicity of the metropolis. In fact this landscape of words records Jewish inhabitants of Berlin who disappeared into the concentration camps. Libeskind is driven beyond architecture as commonly understood by the urgency of his message, driven by a desperate historical situation to give buildings meanings they inherently can't carry. He revives the old idea of the building as a text, as even a single letter, a concept with more power in Hebrew tradition perhaps than any other, a culture which encoded itself not in images but the more portable figures of language. So when he comes to decipher the most profound results of the most searing experience Libeskind returns to a form of reading, and expects that the most wrenching and involving building will already be *written* in the fabric of the city and will only require that he strengthen its lines to become visible to all.

To skeptics the process remains deeply implausible. They look at the building whose form seems utterly arbitrary, unlike other buildings not in showing forth some buried truth about Berlin and its history but in flaunting the private whimsy of the architect. They point to other Libeskind projects with similar zigzag form and no circumstantial connection to the Holocaust. This division of view is not easily repairable. No one can deny the highly intellectual nature of this design, and to some it will seem inappropriate that meanings so pressing should be formulated with such deliberation.

Against this complaint one can only say that there is a venerable tradition of oblique and zigzag approaches to truth. Far-fetched and intricate formulations which keep some of us outside the mystery are to others the most effective spurs to plumbing it. Libeskind's museum will eventually be a powerful spatial experience promulgating certain meanings. It is also already, and will continue to be when built, a written fragment or remnant of a missing inscription which can be pieced together from afar by many who will never set foot in Berlin.

7

Politics

This chapter could be called "Architecture and Oppression," for it takes a predominantly negative view of its subject, focusing on buildings as a means of intimidation and control. Certainly this does not exhaust the significance of politics in architecture, but concentrating on the architectural efforts of rulers exposes among other things an awful consistency in the regimes most concerned to memorialize themselves in built form.

Though generally a political thrust will be obvious in the examples, we begin with a few where it is not. To us the Gothic Temple in the eighteenth-century landscape gardens at Stowe doesn't look political, but contemporaries knew it as the Temple of Liberty. They thought it reasonable to express political sentiments in gardens and interpreted this irregular and backward-looking building as a partisan statement. Gothic was English—a native, independent, even Whig style. English gardens were unfettered as against French, and were furthermore apt places for those in political opposition to express their wilder resentments and dissatisfactions. Gibbs's Gothic is one of the furthest reaches of this spirit and sits appropriately at considerable distance from the house.

Gothic was subversive at Stowe, but at Oxford it had an almost opposite, ultraconservative significance. Hawksmoor's preferred design for All Souls was classical and his Gothic version is stiff and reluctant, all prongs and pinnacles and towers, with thinly disguised Venetian windows lurking underneath. Like certain country houses of slightly later date, it combines picturesque exteriors with classical decor indoors. In spite of this unprincipled stylistic opportunism, Gothic at Oxford already corresponds to an unhealthy interest in antiquity and tradition: disguising oneself in the past signifies resistance to change.

Hawksmoor's towers ended taller and spindlier than his earlier proposals and thus more trivially picturesque. Ordinarily, towers recur in heavily politicized architecture as a serious form of intimidation. At Sabaudia, the Mussolini new town in the Pontine Marshes, there is no shortage of them, yet they mean something different from their blustering sense in normative Fascist new towns nearby. While paying lip service to the rules of Fascist propaganda, the young architects who won the Sabaudia commission managed to insert a version of modernism in which towers are almost pure aesthetic abstractions.

Yet the center of their diminutive made-up city is oversupplied with public buildings. Three competing centers of power are signaled by three towers, the town hall, the party building, and, sidelined in its own secondary square, the church.

Modernism remained problematic even in these years when it seemed to have a chance to become the official Fascist mode. Thus, a battle with the provincial party chief over the height of the tallest tower at Sabaudia could only be settled by a special visit of the great aesthetic arbiter, Mussolini, who came down this time on the side of formalist proportion as against literal niceties of propaganda. The two impulses are balanced at Sabaudia, generalized modernist harmonies and monumental inflation concealed in the interlocking plan.

Terragni's Project A/B for the Palazzo Littorio in Rome, devised in collaboration with Cattaneo and Lingeri, also turns modernist forms to ceremonial purposes. The main element on the elevation to the street is a huge curved wall or screen suspended from steel trusses and coated in porphyry. Lines of stress are sketched across the surface in aluminum inlay, and this hardheaded structural diagram lends a kind of dazzling glitter to the huge cape of imperial purple which frames a high rostrum breaking the curve at its center. All the architectural novelty serves only to create a backdrop for the Leader's rare appearances high above the adoring crowds, who form a key feature of the perspectives submitted with the competition entry. Terragni's forms are innovative but the functions catered to are extremely retrograde—shrines to the Fascist dead, a party headquarters, and, clinching it all, this altar for the elevation of the ruler which stays empty most days in the year.

In Terragni's earlier designs it still remains an active question how far Mussolini and modernism are truly intertwined and whether the propaganda might not be changed or disappear leaving the architecture intact: how easily could this architecture free itself from this politics? In a meeting room in the Casa del Fascio at Como only one fragment of reality interrupts the abstract mural by Radice, a life-size standing photograph of the Duce addressing the meeting in surrogate form. Like the towers at Sabaudia this is a rather subtle affront but perhaps all the more disturbing for perverting a vocabulary we regard as neutral into a partisan statement.

The Soviet government also felt the need to qualify modernist architecture with moralizing representational art. Twenty-five years after the end of the war they erected a monument in what used to be the center of Riga to the Latvian Riflemen, leftist partisans who hid in the forests and harassed the Germans. Between the monolith and the surviving city stands a wall of a building, unwindowed and giving no sign of its purpose. This is an extremely uninviting museum dedicated to the Latvian Riflemen, another case of modernism put to unliberating uses. In earlier decades the counterposed sculpture would probably have been a memorial to the Red Army; now it gives cautious permission to local pride, but symbolizes these unruly bands in inert form: three partisans have grown together into a Cerberus pillar which faces in every direction without a trace of movement.

The monument and museum occupy what was formerly one of the densest parts of the old city, bombed and then completely cleared after the war. Now it signifies the removal, not the salvage of history. The monument stands in an empty plain, and behind it, cutting us off from the city and the past, the wall of the museum forms a barricade we cannot see through or easily think our way around. The net effect of this complex of 1969–1970 is to make us feel hopeless about any continuity between pre- and post-war experience, as if the designer's brief had been to try to show that the memory of what it was like in pre-Soviet times is useless in practical terms.

A larger exercise in shutting people off from their experience, the wall which went up overnight in 1961 between the two halves of Berlin, was one of the great constructive feats of the century. For twenty-eight years it caused a profound deformation in the life of the city, but perhaps it only made more inescapable an underlying political reality. Now that the Wall is gone, existing only in memorial fragments some of which have been turned into art works; now that formerly unthinkable journeys are possible and new transport links are being built, the presence of the Wall is fading though perhaps less quickly than we might have anticipated. Now we credit the Wall with all the still-evident differences between East and West Berlin.

The Berlin Wall was a fascinating example of an arbitrary work of architecture, like Christo's *Running Fence* or Eisenman's brutal geometry. It cut through buildings and streets and thus exposed the raw nerves and charred flesh of the city more effectively, so for several decades it was the best place in the world to see the perverse effects of political conflict on ordinary lives.

In the 1970s during a long wait while one's passport was fingered in another room one could examine a little display extolling the humanity of the puppet Wilhelm Pieck, to whom children were shown presenting flowers in dingy photos against a background of harsh blue cloth in the folds of which were placed a few loaves of bread to signify the abundance we would find inside the Wall.

A wall is one of the most incontrovertible statements a ruler can make, yet it often signifies a certain weakness or vulnerability. Hadrian's Wall across northern England is no longer politically controversial of course. Now it is regarded as scenic and used by schoolchildren for outings. Formerly it looked different from the two sides, like the one in Berlin known in the East as the Anti-Fascist Barricade, keeping Western corruption out, not Eastern prisoners in. Like the Berlin Wall, Hadrian's was a massive imposition when built, tearing the country in two.

The Edwardian castles which made a kind of wall around Wales were among the most brutal assertions of dominance ever, yet the designer of Caernarvon Castle still found time for crystalline geometry and colored banding in the exterior stonework reminiscent of brick-stone amalgams in the defenses of Constantinople. In Constantinople these were the usual materials of public buildings; in Wales the device is less practical and more purely aesthetic.

In East Berlin in the 1950s the most prestigious building project took the form of walls of housing on either side of a long ceremonial avenue named after the new country's Friend to the east. Whatever else the massy buildings of Stalinallee (which became Karl-Marxallee in 1961) may have been, they were barricades or defenses of the new system which needed to legitimize itself. These assertions of the new life under socialism are full of archaisms and conservative gestures, like towers which recur at intervals to punctuate the monotony and also to express a domineering impulse not that far from warlike motifs at Caernarvon.

Workers on these quarters for the new Party elite, pushed to Stakhonovite feats of endurance and production, sparked off the riots of 1953, first signs that the workers' state might not be serving the workers very well. Such hiccups in the realization of this socialist pomp were later glossed over when Berlin was promoted as a *modern* capital, whose finest architectural gestures depended on regressive classicism not so different from Hitler's. Now many of the prestigious shops along the avenue are vacant, the ceramic facing is falling off, the gold of the anodized balustrades grows dull; the dream is a ruin.

Stalinallee isn't remarkable for its decay, which could have happened anywhere, but for falling short of boasts which could admit only ascent, not decline. Name changes were among the earliest indicators of defeat—a society which falls out from under the spell of its own heroes is becoming precarious. Perhaps the first signs of instability should be located earlier—in the wholesale renaming of the streets of Berlin in 1947 after socialist heroes, martyrs, and time servers—Otto Grotewohl, Wilhelm Pieck, Klement Gottwald, Rosa Luxemburg, and many others—they are a catalogue of the great and less than great, all of whom are lessened when they become the stuffing of partisan utterance and are claimed as the property of decrepit rulers to brandish as they please.

The intention of partisan street names is to make even the city fabric declare its allegiance and to prevent anyone, friend or foe, from going anywhere or saying anything about the journey without seeming to endorse a particular political administration. The trouble is that this wonderfully simple device has a way of backfiring: users do not forget; the new names remain irritants, and the old ones smolder underneath. At the first opportunity almost two generations later, Leningrad isn't Leningrad anymore.

It is instructive to look at some of the blunders great architects fall into when they ordain things on the scale of Stalinallee. The greatest stupidity of Stalinallee is missing: there are no stylistic hangovers in Le Corbusier's Plan Voisin of 1925 for the complete restructuring of central Paris. It is doubtful that Corb really believed the old core of the city could be entirely swept away to be replaced by his enormous cross-shaped blocks with empty spaces between. Placing his new city there, as he does in a series of powerful perspective drawings, is probably just a way of getting greater attention for his ideas. But no matter how hypothetical one takes certain details to be, the proposal is extremely intimidating in allowing the architect's will such scope and limiting variety so severely.

Equally grandiose proposals came from Mies van der Rohe just before he left Germany, when he still imagined an accommodation with Nazi power might be possible. His Reichsbank project of 1933 is based on the heartless repetition of identical huge units glued into a common base and mitigated, but not much, by giving a curved edge to the whole.

Mies carries over authoritarian sorts of planning to new situations. Though his first large commission in America, the IIT campus, eschews the heaviness of these last German projects, it achieves unity by a numbing consistency. Deflections from an overall grid in the plan are a saving subtlety, but never sacrifice symmetry in the individual pieces.

Socialists came back to Berlin after the war trailing a new ideology but soon found themselves reusing Goering's Air Ministry with minimal cosmetic detoxification. Like the American reemployment of the rocket scientist Wernher von Braun, this seems more than an amusing historical curiosity. The main visible means of salving consciences over the transfer was an optimistic mural fired on ceramic tile, now in disrepair. Under that gloomy arcade it depicts a joyous procession of workers like the animals entering the ark, every one with a generic or social identity. They come in groups and dress, if not quite in uniform, recognizably and similarly. Colors are sober and strong, and gestures mechanical: raised arms to signal happiness, handshakes for community. Doubts arise: the semiformal march suggests servitude, not happiness. Though the roles are different, it is a modulation within the same register as Nazi parades, familiar from films and railway station murals which prescribe just as much as they celebrate.

The orchestration of large crowds is not peculiar to twentieth-century politics, of course. Rulers have always been able to command such uniformity for more or less benign or trivial purposes. Even a bit of pageantry like the War of Beauty staged in Florence in 1616 and recorded in Jacques Callot's etchings was in its way a serious demonstration of power. The Nazi rallies (especially the annual Party Days in Nuremberg) were almost the high point of the regime, frightening opponents and intimidating those citizens on the verge of opposition.

In architectural settings crowds are often represented by selected heroic individuals with strong generic content. Mukhina's *Collective Farm Laborer* (female) *and Factory Worker* (male) embody the whole nation and cover many categories, male/female, country/town, old/new. They wield their tools like weapons and carry the spectator along in the forward rush of their enthusiasm.

One would dearly like to know what feelings such propaganda rouses in various segments of the population. On the brick flank of a 1950s polytechnic in Györ, Hungary, a group in stone is silhouetted, a young man with a hammer and a young woman with a book. They look in robust health, the human equivalent of tanks or jeeps, with clunky builds and clothes to match. The book is brandished even more aggressively than the hammer, like a permanent placard daring someone to take it down. How many observers would have identified with these figures? And are certain groups pointedly excluded by them? It seems possible the sculptures mainly functioned to polarize the community and, paradoxical as it seems associated with an educational institution, that this is a veiled attack on intellectuals.

Such sculptural posters bring to mind the large slogans which decorated the skyline on top of many public buildings in Moscow as recently as the early 1980s. To Western visitors the self-congratulation in these watchwords sometimes seemed childish. "Hail to the Great Soviet People," "All Praise to the Communist Party of the Soviet Union." Was there ever a population so suggestible it could believe such mutterings? There didn't need to be. However much you disbelieved, you acknowledged the power which put the messages in place. Public advertising in the West may not be vastly different; it hides in irony, but there is still the crass measure of how much space it takes.

Socialist Realist sculpture and architecture give a special prominence to manual labor, but it has been a loaded subject for centuries. When George Stubbs painted *The Haymakers* (dated 1785), which converts backbreaking fieldwork into a harmonious dance, who was it serving? Was it pacifying workers by idealizing their labor? But transforming their simple white clothing into luminous spiritual substance would hardly convince them. The intended hearers for the sermon on simplicity are the masters: the painting makes other people's labor more bearable.

By comparison with Boucher's pastoral Stubbs looks hardheaded. Boucher's peasants are wonderfully out of touch, immune to any distress that harsh weather or poverty might bring. When he shows Madame de Pompadour outdoors, she is camouflaged just as effectively by lace as she could ever be by tatters. To understand such a picture we must know what it is reacting against. Remembering Versailles, where it is the hardest commodity to find, we understand the premium which came to be placed on simplicity. Appended to the palace is a whole city of greenery. Though they try to conceal the fact, these gardens are one of the most highly regulated of all human organizational feats. It is entirely alien to the spirit of the garden to remember how many of the soldiers who excavated the lake west of the palace died of malaria bred by the swampy conditions, but such extensive orchestrations always bespeak immense power to command people's movements.

There are few images which convey this very well for Versailles, nothing as vivid as the representations of a Renaissance pope's project to move the Egyptian obelisk into a central position in front of St. Peter's. Contemporary prints of this event show the armies of precisely deployed lifters all of whom were sworn to silence so that commands would ring out clearly. A laborer who cried out to warn that one of the ropes needed wetting before it burst into flames came very near being executed for the crime of speaking. To us the expenditure of effort in this project seems colossal, but it made a significant and economical cultural statement: the Pope by moving this one piece of stone overruled and digested the belief systems of the past.

The city of Washington is focused on another obelisk, the Washington Monument, which sits at the center of a Versailles-like disposition of greenery and buildings. The park setting is a kind of camouflage, for all is highly regulated with meanings precisely worked out. The scope for symbolic expression, i.e., propaganda, is very great, and these are political proclamations of an unassailable kind: for the structure of this government appears to be in tune with the natural world.

The plan of Washington is notable for combining centralizing and radial impulses. Its subtlety is perhaps to allow for multiple centers of political power, but there can be no doubt that a power field is being laid out. And aerial views quickly confirm that the result thus far is a bureaucratic if not an architectural nightmare.

Among the clearest examples of architecture as the controller of personal destinies are Ledoux's large projects dating from around the time of the inception of Washington, where rigid order is ordained by a grid plan whose spaciousness only facilitates stricter control. In the planned village of Maupertuis the farmers would have enjoyed a pleasant but utterly unfree life, watched over by the all-seeing eye of the police, directed out from a perfect sphere of masonry sitting in a square hole and reached by stairs suspended over the void. Houses in this community are separated from each other by alarming blank spaces, but conform dutifully to a rigid geometrical alphabet. One could obtain a similar effect by spacing sugar cubes sparsely on a table top. Though the units are the cells of a hive they are separated from each other by considerable distances, alienated but not truly independent, like residents in a typical suburb.

Ledoux's system of *barrières* or gates for Paris is almost to give each of the integers at Maupertuis a specific place and purpose, turning the grid into a necklace. He threw himself enthusiastically into the project of imagining a series of strong forms with almost no content. One of the most interesting, which remained unbuilt, hollows out the volume to produce a negative image of the building. Concave sides threaten to meet in a wasp waist, while pedimented ends are reduced to inhabited pillars at the corners and empty space under the roof ridge: from the simple figure we arrive at its skeleton by a process of subtraction.

Even supposedly socialist housing projects show an appetite for coercive order, but of course, as Ledoux was aware, orchestrating private spaces gives the greatest opportunity for oppressive control of the lives of citizens. Nowa Huta near the ancient capital of Krakow in Poland was the display piece of Communist propaganda in the 1950s, a new town for the workers employed at a gigantic steel mill, an archetypal instance of Stalin's preference for heavy industry. The residential sectors of Nowa Huta are based on wide boulevards and massive blocks which converge on a central square, now no more than a meeting place for buses and trams. Repetitive forms and inhuman scale make their effect before one notices the classical trimmings, sometimes pompous, sometimes whimsical. By a strange twist of history, these workers' dwellings are dignified by giving them Versailles-like magnitude and grandeur. In the 1920s luxurious Western villas borrowed their architectural language from (proletarian) factories; then in the 1950s aristocratic palaces provided the model for mass housing in Eastern Europe. In the interiors of these buildings today the pompous pretense isn't maintained, and the hallways of this showpiece are as dingy and crumbling as in the bedraggled cut-rate work of later decades, as if the standard of upkeep is different inside and out, making this a true Potemkin village.

Approaching the steel mill at Nowa Huta, one steps suddenly further into the past just before the great outburst of modernity in the industrial installation itself. A pair of administration buildings outside the main gates of the plant adopt Renaissance features from nearby Krakow, including fancy battlements, arcades, and courtyards. The point is to give a Polish stamp to the most alien element in the whole scheme, an unsuitable type of industry. Local if bizarre architectural motifs are a way of claiming that Poland wants and welcomes what is in reality a brutal imposition. In Poland the pendulum has swung so far that it is now popularly believed that Nowa Huta was not only placed here as a political counterweight to traditional and conservative Krakow, but that it is upwind of the older city by deliberate intention so that its poisonous fumes will attack the buildings of Krakow, a result which has occurred but was probably not foreseen.

The idea of palaces for the people, so liable to perversion, has a lengthy history. It goes back at least as far as workers' clubs of the 1920s by Melnikov and others, and then later to the local entries in the Palace of the Soviets competition of 1932. Melnikov's proposal for the competition is a frightening conflation of two incompatible forms, an arena and a pyramid, a setting for spectacles and a tomb. On its backside, integrated with huge supports for tiers of offices, are straining colossi. We read their anguish as discomfort with gigantism as a popular form. These and most other Heroes of Socialist Labor are really emissaries of authoritarian ideas, both the slaves and the bodyguards of power.

There had been a hopeful moment as recently as seven years before, but the political situation was volatile and changed rapidly. In 1924 Melnikov won a competition for the Soviet Pavilion at the Paris Exhibition with a design aggressively unstable and dynamic. The building was riven in two by its circulation, a way of saying that the society which produced it put exploratory process ahead of finished result. If the concept was radical, Melnikov's means were simple, almost primitive—lightweight timber and glass construction well within Russian technical capacity. The example is aberrant of course, a temporary erection for foreign consumption where the embarrassment of new ideas wouldn't linger.

Much of the best architectural energy of the time was too impatient for enduring constructions, and a disrupted economy wasn't capable of supporting them anyway. Graphic products like Rodchenko's covers for *Lef* magazine in the 1920s give the full measure of the raw energy and diversity of Soviet visual culture in those years. Here is freedom in an important sense of the word, in a world which for the time being is very unrulebound.

Already the way was being prepared for the weirdly dubbed "socialist realism" in architecture, which meant an antimodernist form of classicism with incongruous vernacular or nationalist trimmings. This reached its full flower after the Second World War in the famous wedding cake or *Zuckerbäckerstil* towers which secretly emulated US skyscrapers but tried to disguise this with statues, murals in sgrafitto, and terminal crests sometimes derived from onion domes or seventeenth-century Russian spires. Moscow is the heartland of these structures but subsidiary examples are dotted across Eastern Europe. For gross signals of opulence and density of uplifting imagery—serious, cheerful murals at every turn—few bourgeois works can equal the International Hotel in Prague. But the main university building in Moscow in the Lenin (formerly Sparrow) Hills is on a vastly greater scale and the hieratic symmetry and formality consequently much more imposing. In the short space of twenty years this society has gone from experimentation to commemoration, from the exploding bomb to the unshakable tomb. To the new student approaching the Babelian monolith it must have seemed that growth and change were finished and that the most one could hope for was to colonize a crevice as high up as one could manage on the unfeeling hide of the behemoth. The university complex depicts the body politic as rigid, rank-oriented, and totally unresponsive. All but the most intrepid will be chastened into inactivity.

It is all too easy for us to explain how the Soviet university got this way. But when we turn to new building at the University of London in the interwar period, there's considerable similarity in scale and form. Senate House was designed by Charles Holden in 1932 and finished before the war. It is virtually the only part completed of a vast plan to carpet Bloomsbury with parallel ranks of gray hulks, a monotony from which the tower would offer the only relief. Though sparsely dotted with plinths which cry out for monumental sculpture, Holden's tower lacks the narrative bombast of the Moscow University buildings. Nonetheless it remains discomforting that these two institutions share the powerful, inappropriate form of the tower.

Like Melnikov, Holden had earlier shown an allegiance to the cylinder and to dynamic ideas of society as mobile, flexible, and increasingly open, above all in new stations for London Transport's expansion into the outer suburbs. These were commissioned and overseen by a chief executive who believed in the liberating potential of public transport and were informed by architectural tours in Holland and Scandinavia.

A more radical version of progressive social ideas in British architecture of the 1930s, with more explicitly Russian inspiration, can be seen in the work of Bertold Lubetkin. His Finsbury Health Centre of 1938 incorporates many functions in one complex—clinic, lecture hall, disinfecting rooms, and morgue—and clearly reflects Melnikov's clubs. Lubetkin uses some of the same devices for suggesting movement and change, expanding pie-shaped forms which are finally pieces of circles. Perhaps the most abstract use of the form is in Lissitzky's famous poster of 1919–1920 where the Red Wedge represents the Soviet Army and the moribund Whites are portrayed as a pale circle.

Like many other progressive Western architects Lubetkin entered the Palace of the Soviets competition. His entry was a monstrous conglomerate of bubble domes and spreading wedges, forms which turn up in his later public housing, above all in the stairwell at Bevin Court which puts an intricate triangle of ramps in a large cylinder. This carries a full charge of symbolic, even propagandist intention, presenting as it does a theatrical vision of social interdependence.

The project had a mildly checkered history. It began as Lenin Court with a little shrine in the foyer incorporating a bust of its namesake. Lubetkin had a number of these made as they kept being defaced or destroyed. Finally in 1946 under heavy political pressure the name was changed from Lenin to Bevin, after the Labour Minister of Housing, a strong anti-Stalinist.

By now Lubetkin's buildings have lost their political valency for most people. No one defaces their logos, or at least no more than any others. Political significance is seldom stamped indelibly on architecture, and easily comes loose. To me a facade like the seventeenth-century church of S. Filippo Neri at Bevagna in

Umbria seemed an archetype of benign and mellow presence. But in Danilo Dolci's book about poverty in Sicily the church is a truly hateful force trying to kill thought before it takes place. Such a text makes one wonder if an outsider—in space or time or both— can ever be very exact in catching the political nuances of buildings: tools of oppression wear for the serious visitor's eyes the soothing aspect of the devoted parent.

8

The **Sacred**

In any general history of architecture, the majority of structures illustrated will be religious buildings in some sense of the term, until partway into the eighteenth century at least. The shift away from the sacred in the West over the last two centuries has been one of the most striking developments in our history, and still continues. In contemporary work sacred purposes are often served in buildings not easily recognized as religious in character.

The category of the sacred includes a wide variety of attempts to put human beings in touch with a higher or more comprehensive reality than they find in their everyday selves. They may think the world is ruled by one or more supernatural beings, or by laws or forces of which they should take some note, to which they should pay some devotion. However rare such feelings have become, historically they are not exceptional. Just because we are striving to look beyond our limitations, it will be more than usually obvious that our choice of examples to illustrate this topic is culture-bound and parochial.

Starting with primitive artifacts means among other things ones which are not well understood. Stonehenge has inspired various interpretations, but the absence of any written record of the builders' intention means that our theories are difficult to agree on or prove. All we are sure of is that the complex was unroofed, an instrument with celestial implications used to decipher forces beyond the earth which regulate light and the seasons. We assume that Salisbury Plain is a place which would always have made one aware of human smallness in the larger scheme of things.

A strong sense of sacred *place* is not a special feature of Christianity over the last few centuries. In English towns and villages most churches sit next to big houses or near the center of settlements. When you find a church isolated in a field, as at Tixover in Rutland, it may mean its village has moved or that the building occupies an earlier pre-Christian holy site, perhaps near a spring or a large burial mound.

Holdovers are a particular feature of early churches. Old locations, old motifs—Romanesque buildings all over Europe are treasuries of pagan material, usually well mixed with later elements. We are likely to exaggerate the antiquity of the stave churches of Norway for this reason. They bristle with pagan reminders, dragons' heads like ship's prows or demon scarers, and carved expanses of the old interlace, now interpreted as the snares of this world. In these tiered wooden cakes there is little sign of the classical inheritance of Christianity.

In other outlying areas like England you will find carved portrayals of events which took place in Roman provinces—like the Three Kings before Herod at Bishopsteignton in Devon—whose carvers had probably never seen a classical sculpture in their lives. These squat figures with their huge eyes and heavy robes might be Sumerian or Celtic, a Christian story as filtered through a pre-Christian mind. But then new religions are usually overlays on older ones and often give unexpected glimpses into unplaceable darkness.

The earliest surviving Christian buildings in Britain often seem regressions from what went before. Anglo-Saxon structures like Escomb church in County Durham frequently incorporate tailored Roman stones into their crude and pinched but somehow spiritual proportions. To skeptical observers these buildings will seem miserable underlit barns with rude beast heads thrusting out from the wall as if against some strong current in the ether. To more sympathetic eyes the high narrow spaces suggest powerful if technologically unsophisticated aspiration, examples of immersion in the sacred as a kind of backsliding or regression to more primitive stages. It has been more common than we readily admit for sacred buildings to incorporate profound contradictions, such as reminders of previous, antagonistic cults or motives like fortification and defense which we regard as incompatible with religion.

Is it even possible to look for standard sacred configurations? Are there universal constituents which invariably make a sacred space? Or can we at least delineate a basic Western one which derives from classical models and is focused on the most distant wall from the point of entry? To enumerate the constituents of this planar composition, we might look at one of the oldest examples, a late Roman shrine converted to Christian use like the Tempietto del Clitunno near Spoleto. Here we find an elaborate niche with a smaller aedicule in it, like a flattened miniature temple. Over the round arch of the niche is a triangular pediment, which declares the space over again as a focus and a concentration. This shrine was built to commemorate a sacred spring and later picked up its connection with a female martyr. Then in a later phase the architectural elements got surrounded with narrative and documentary frescoes.

This simple arrangement contains the germ of elements later much elaborated, like the altar and the apse, both a frontal and a receding gatherer of meditative gazes, the flat component more cerebral, the nestlike enclosed space more appealing to the senses.

We can find the same elements repeated at diverse scales and in a range of forms from the most naive and improvised to the most lavish and long meditated. Street shrines in Braga (or almost anywhere in the Latin South) include the essentials of this type of sacred space in rudimentary form. They are based on a boxlike frame in tin which makes a little room, furnished with a decorative fringe keeping the spectator at a distance like a chancel screen. Within is a focal image surrounded by lights and flowers, symbolic representatives of different forms of vital energy.

The whole construction is based on the premise that worship has to direct itself somewhere, in this case to a point above eye level. Raising your eyes to pray to this image is a confirmation in spatial terms of the relation religion is built on. All of architecture's efforts to reinforce a sense of the sacred are only an elaboration of these basic constituents. The experience can be a great deal vaster, richer, and more complicated but remains essentially the same.

In an interior like Santos Passos in Guimarães the senses will often get waylaid on the path to the altar, though the profusion of forms and the variety of materials are only multiplications of the ideas of frame and fringe. Here there is the added twist of flamboyantly secular motifs and substances, an intellectually significant stage in the desertion of the sacred which characterizes both Catholic and Protestant designs of the eighteenth century. At Guimarães tiled walls make the church seem part of a fragile dinner service and gold makes the impression lighter though not in the least immaterial. Walls are turned to screens or theater backdrops and we seem to have entered an intimate space like a bedroom. This sensation must partly derive from the veiled and half-disclosed vistas, and partly from the resemblance of the final shrine to a great four-poster bed with piled caskets where the sleepers would be.

Externally the church is a giant version of the shrine on the altar, like a tall narrow cabinet framed by ornamented posts which offers a concatenation of doorlike openings far outstripping any actual need or possibility of entry. Here too are many incongruous motifs and materials, spiritually speaking—garden urns, balconies (a kind of canopy in reverse), frills like clothing and tiled surfaces like small objects on a dressing table. However complex the composition becomes, it remains somewhat static, holding itself aloof from and above the observer.

There's a whole other conception of sacred space which doesn't lead you to an image or a screen, which doesn't culminate in however awesome a flat panel on which you focus for meditation, but contrarily puts you under a dome in a more or less circular space that you can position yourself at the center of. This space affects you through its very existence, not through what is in it. So we cannot claim that this centralized idea is an immaterial one, for the space is actual after all, but rather that the effect is not dependent on surface qualities, though it may combine with distracting or muted richness. The plan of the little Dientzenhofer church at Dobra Voda in Bohemia appears an archetypal example of this kind of geometry, based on a circle struggling for freedom of expression within a rectangle, which threatens to collapse into negatives of a circle.

Even on the exterior at Dobra Voda these clear geometrical themes are obscured by pediments, urns, and statues which bend the simple identities of geometrical solids this way and that. In fact this architect is no longer satisfied with the simple identities of spaces: a cylinder becomes most interesting as it begins to be submerged or lost in a flat wall.

One of the great examples of a centralized space pure and undiluted is the chamber under the great dome of Hagia Sophia in Istanbul. The exterior of this building must have looked even more factorylike before the windows in its vertical flanks were partly filled in to strengthen the earthquake-damaged fabric. Thus the general impression of a piled-up city of separate parts was increased. Now along with a certain clumsiness goes the Babel-like ascent to impossible heights. The nearby St. Irene, also of sixth-century date, may give a clearer idea of the basic structural system, but a heaped complexity has become inseparable from the idea of Hagia Sophia.

The interior is what this building really exists for, ingeniously approached through misleading or deflecting cross-spaces of high narrow proportions (the double narthex) which expel you unprepared under the great domed space. At the east in the profusion of semi-domes we get some idea how the climb into the heavens is achieved, but essentially this is a building which is there all at once, suddenly.

Hagia Sophia is another example of the use of a sacred site and envelope by a later cult, but this space could swallow almost any fitting until it had very little impact on the real experience. The most obtrusive signs of the building's five centuries as a mosque are the largest, latest, and hardest to remove, the great green discs inscribed with pious prayers in gold script in the nineteenth century.

The incongruity of these is geometric not cultural. In no other mosque is there a decorative element which conflicts so starkly with the surrounding geometry and scale. Arabic inscriptions could easily be accommodated in Hagia Sophia as they are in other churches become mosques, but not on this scale and not in roundels, or in roundels hung just below the springing of the arch. The magnificence of a large being is not well conveyed by his name in letters too big for their surroundings.

As usual, some Christian images were whited out or even destroyed at the time of the conversion. Of course it would be good to recover the diffuse richness which the mosaic covering would have given. Where the covering survives in the galleries one loses oneself in soft surfaces like crusty velvet. Still, the erased images never played a very prominent part in the total impression, and the nineteenth-century fakes in ochre paint are a surprisingly good substitute.

In SS. Sergius and Bacchus, Hagia Sophia's much smaller contemporary, the incongruity of later, Islamic decoration is even more aggravated but charming as well. Above rich late Roman capitals and cornice in marble are rococo fringes in soft blue paint. These are the colors and motifs—stylized plants, borders like settings for precious stones—which turn up in Iznik tiles, with which whole walls were covered in mosques built from scratch.

Was it sympathy with the prior non-Islamic sensibility which made them draw back from imposing the powerful two-dimensional world of the tiles on the intricate spatial articulation of Sergius and Bacchus? The alternative chosen has its overtones of frivolity, as if one had turned a Bavarian stuccoist loose in an early Christian basilica.

Conversion from church to mosque in Istanbul usually requires a slight reorientation, to adjust from facing east to facing Mecca, with a result surprisingly like Deconstructivist architecture overlaying a new concept on a preexisting reality. Islam sets itself minimally but precisely at odds with the world it finds itself in, an attitude not applied consistently throughout the whole building but only at the apse end and along the eastern wall. Besides the reorientation there is the insertion of sub-buildings within the building, most noticeably the pulpit with its steep approach, mounting which one climbs a tower whose peaked cap presents an absurd picture of a mountaintop puncturing heaven, or at least the air held captive under the dome.

Anyone familiar with the usual furniture of churches is also aware of what has been removed: this is a body stripped and reclothed: particularly the thick coating of carpets has a powerful, womblike effect; one is less inclined to stand and is consequently more dwarfed by one's surroundings.

In Spain the contrary process occurs: mosques reused as churches; so Cordoba's is given the rudiments of a Baroque exterior and a roughly inserted nave. In neither conversion is the alien context quite obliterated, and the reorientation within it continues to occur even now whenever one chooses to notice it.

The main Byzantine sacred format, a centralized domed plan with peripheral galleries, became almost obligatory in the grandest Turkish mosques and also turns up in the small mosques of Sinan, the great Turkish Renaissance architect probably of Greek extraction. The symbolism of these spaces still fits, though differing from its sense in the Christian source. Some will be tempted to claim that these adaptations prove the universal power of well-devised architectural concepts. Others will lament the unnatural flexibility of creeds which by convenient reinterpretation can make themselves at home in borrowed garments, as if function took precedence over ideology.

Many of the great religious controversies have centered on questions of how literal or abstract or metaphorical one could be in interpreting the injunctions of a sacred text or the implications of an architectural form. Islam maintains literal attachments which have weakened and almost disappeared in the West. Abstract, map-like representations of specific holy spaces in Mecca are a constant of Islamic art which turn up on tiles and carpets and reveal a kind of attachment to particular earthly places which was more common in the West in the Middle Ages. Replicas and pilgrimages then formed a much larger part of religious life than they do now.

Controversy still surrounds the question of how helpful or how true things and images of things can be in coming close to God. Sometimes it is hard to separate a solicitude for physical remnants like the chairs saints sat in and the bones they sat with from exhibitions of worldly wealth and power. Naive credulity and worldly shrewdness have sometimes converged in the history of Christianity, and lavish depictions have become potent weapons in the hands of authority.

Many have stumbled over what Bernini did with Peter's chair. This simple piece of equipment had eventually assumed an inordinate significance. The cathedra or seat from which the bishop made his pronouncements was the germ from which the cathedral, the chair's magnificent architectural garment or housing, sprang. From St. Peter's chair in Rome were controlled an expanding network of other chairs, nodes of physical power all over Europe. Peter sat on wood on the floor. By Bernini's time to express the expansive power of this seat or locus it was floated many feet above the ground, hidden in metal and surrounded by clouds of sculpted angels, until it became unlikely that anyone would remember that under the swirling bronze was a simple wooden frame, a pretext long surpassed.

One can turn this dyspeptic vision on many of the finest works of art the church has commissioned, like the iron grilles closing the west porch of Braga cathedral. The contrast between blue metal and gray stone, between Baroque frills and late Gothic corrugations, is diverting until one thinks to ask: who is the church protecting itself from, and how has it come to seem natural that it should own so many things that it fears for their safety and wants to give an impression of impregnable power?

There is the problem of the church as a worldly power, and as what kind of power? In the 1960s a self-declared bishop wearing a cheap gold robe and (after the ceremony) a paper crown went around the campuses of small American colleges crowning himself "King of the World, for Good." Perhaps he was not as silly as he sounds: he knew that Christ's "kingdom" hadn't come, yet seemed to think he could speed it up by a simple attention-getting device. To what extent he hoped real power would fall into his hands, like Sancho Panza in a waking dream, is hard to say.

The church as an owner, landlord, or exploiter and the physical paraphernalia of kingship or worship—robes for Christ or dioramas of moments in his life—how deep is the connection? There is a complicated history which culminates in the sacred mounts like Varallo or Varese in northern Italy and Bom Jesus near Braga in Portugal where a penitential climb is punctuated by devotional scenes in which three-dimensional images are life-size or nearly, spaces between them are literal, and exaggerated lighting is used to catch you off guard. Does the liking for physical replicas signal a superior faith, or a kind of decline? The devotee's attention can only be caught or held by the most garish means, only a step away from horror films which show axes descending and bleeding stumps. In aesthetes' acceptance of such effects it is variously argued that the senses are only a route toward something else, or, contrarily, that such sensuous displays evince healthy acceptance of our earthly plight, with which these tableaux have come to terms more successfully than the idealists and Puritans who continue to find this literalism crass or degrading.

There is of course another tradition which keeps the images without the literalism. Its best exemplars are those hypnotic Byzantine Madonnas, standing out against their gold backgrounds, inhabiting their strange thrones which look like walled cities or Roman arenas, condensed images of the whole encircling world in which the Christ child is half sunk as in a well. Corresponding to these two vastly different images are two kinds of architectural space: the standoffish Byzantine and the importunate Baroque.

Protestantism was an attempt to get out from under the power of images as well as the worldly power of the Church. The blank white walls of eighteenth-century English churches with no distracting side altars mean freedom not starvation seen with the right eyes. But before long Protestantism itself began to be re-Protestantized, with results even more impoverished to an unsympathetic gaze, low on the social scale and called Low Church.

At its best, Methodism is another attempt to escape the physicalization and hence trivialization or sidetracking of Christianity into worldliness. So the typical early chapel, after the enthusiastic gathering has left its open-air origins and moved indoors, is more like a schoolroom than a church, its windows frank and clear, and dark-hued wood its most luxurious substance. But the central position of the pulpit suggests another kind of tyranny. As many novels show, Methodism too has a particular cultural flavor which can be exceedingly narrow, not transcending its physical setting in the back streets of provincial towns. These locations are evocative of a certain kind of obscure existence, unshowy but not always unprideful.

Certain seventeenth-century Portuguese facades in the plain style reveal that the impulses which drove Protestantism were not unknown in Catholic countries. Distrust of the senses takes refuge in flat planes and hard edges, and framed texts replace images. So there is a temperamental Protestantism which doesn't necessarily coincide with sectarian preference. Almost every modernist church is strongly Protestant, whether literally so or not.

Among the most striking examples are two churches designed by Sigurd Lewerentz, a Swede who built little but distinctively. One is not supposed to detect a religious building here. If there is a recognizable code in these buildings, it is taken from industrial structures rather than churches. Lewerentz regresses forcefully to a primitive sense of the materials, but there's an extreme refinement in all his separate decisions to face everything openly, making abstract patterns of surface wiring, clipping windows to walls with no frames, and dramatizing drainage by gnarling the gutters.

The sophisticated primitivism of Lewerentz's designs goes far back in Scandinavia. Gunnar Asplund's Woodland Chapel of several decades earlier is both a chaste temple and a primitive hut, perfect in its proportions and rude in its constituents. Lewerentz too designed a classical chapel in the same place, but as you would expect it is asymmetrical and deeply eccentric in its quiet way, with a portico at right angles to the space and canted slightly. Such aberrations are not immediately apparent, and these buildings are more subversive than they seem at first. Sometimes the goal is a design so recessive that it fades into the trees, like the alignments in the cemetery near these chapels, where spindly trunks of pines form a structure of columns among which the graves are lost or partly hidden. To this way of thinking the most sublime space is one where human intervention is barely sensed, a kind of design which turns a forest into a subtle form of sacred architecture.

Even more invisible design was produced by the Shakers, which is now praised for not looking like design at all but the most efficient practicality. Yet these people were religious fanatics if extremely peaceful ones, who enforced strict separations and abstentions. Married couples joined the sect and lived separately thereafter, sworn to celibacy yet coming together in religious services which were a strange variety of ecstatic dance. Here is a point of contact with dervishes in Islam, abstemious mystics who erupt in ritual dances.

Looked at with minimal knowledge of the minds of the makers, Shaker rooms with all their pegs and boxes, their simple devices for completing household tasks, resemble warehouses, factories, prisons. Modernism learning from factories was perhaps putting itself through a self-purification not so remote from Shaker amputations and denials. Interestingly enough it is the smaller devices, the machines of the Shakers, not larger architectural containers, which attract modern enthusiasm. Their dormitories and workrooms taken as wholes are more evidently the joyless scenes of restriction and denial.

No one has so far suggested shutting anyone up in an art compound, but if this were to be done the modern equivalent of Shaker architecture and design would be the quarters for displaying art which excludes extraneous sensation and surrounds the works with a white void. An institution in Houston goes further than most in producing this effect of the sanctified prison. This is the Rothko chapel on the grounds of the University of St. Thomas, which realizes the dream of Mark Rothko that his paintings should be seen alone where they can expand to fill the viewer's whole visual field.

In practice this metaphysical brief is realized in a formal layout like a Zen garden, with a pool containing gnomic sculpture focused on the windowless chapel, a cube of pale brick. Inside, the visitor is surrounded by a set of Rothko's paintings lit by natural light from above. These are even less sharply defined than his famous lozenge compositions, which stack up two or three colored squares of uncertain edge against a colored background.

In Houston the effect is even more like staring into a deep featureless pool. Here the color hovers somewhere between black and purple and changes imperceptibly toward the edge. The idea comes into one's head that it is a picture of the soul or spiritual plasma presented in the most elemental way. The boundlessness of this experience is at odds with the neat symmetry of the building, a little Mayan temple at the center of a composition like Mondrian on an urban scale. The university has bought up lots of early twentieth-century bungalows on the surrounding streets which are then painted the same gray all over, as if made from a special material or carved from single blocks. The whole enterprise is a reinterpretation of the suburb as a single work of art, and like a Mondrian it is asymmetric in detail but rigorous underneath. This color scheme is one of the most compelling aesthetizations ever, achieved by the simplest physical means but founded on a profound conceptual shift. It is not known how Rothko felt about being at the center of this larger rethinking. He fell out with Philip Johnson, originally commissioned to provide the architectural setting, because the building wasn't properly subordinated to the paintings. His canvases establish within their own borders ruthless subordinations which were apparently not enough; the artist had ambitions to subdue more of the world outside and create a wider surrounding hush for the contemplation of the paintings.

One of Mies van der Rohe's more fantastical projects was a museum for the display of a single work of art, Picasso's *Guernica,* against the backdrop of the Rocky Mountains. These proportions conform to a certain conceptual ideal: painting and architecture evenly matched, played against a striking landscape.

In works like the Farnsworth House Mies's essentialism approaches Rothko's. Before it was intruded on by nearby buildings, this villa did better at creating a sacred stillness, laying out its slender number of forms hieratically. They are suspended above the ground and semitransparent, like hard-edged ghosts or metaphysical propositions rather than ordinary living spaces. Mies's specification of multiple coats of white paint for the steel components might appear to treat the building as an exquisite piece of furniture but was just one element in an overall dematerialization. The white and glittering result, in which everything is tenuously attached to anything else, leaves one in doubt whether it is really there or not.

His earliest venture in essentialism, twenty-five years before, was a glass skyscraper for Friedrichstrasse in Berlin, a utopian idea which appeared at a moment when glass as a mystical material had a certain currency among the German avant-garde. This unbuilt project is uncannily prescient of the other end of Mies's career when he again located the sacred in an unexpected place. At that point he produced large corporate buildings in which he attempted, rather quixotically, with glass and steel made ineffable by painting it black, anodizing it, or arresting rust on it like a patina, to spiritualize commerce and free it from all hint of entanglement in politics or everyday life.

When Giuseppe Terragni came to represent Paradise, the most ineffable of Dante's realms, in his architectural rendition of the *Divine Comedy,* he also chose glass, in quasi-classical format—a hypostyle hall full of simple cylindrical columns. The columns support a grid of slender glass beams, and you see further columns through nearer ones by some peculiar property of spiritual substance. In this world of ghosts two bodies can occupy the same place at the same time. Terragni's most surprising feat is to propound these allegories without compromising the modernist language in which he is comfortable. Unlike Mies's, though, these are frankly useless spaces, a kind of architectural promenade on the way to and from a library.

Of course the brief for this project is heavily ideal, but perhaps there is nonetheless a sweeping truth in these works of Terragni and Mies: that the modernist route to sensations of the sacred leads through abstraction, and that modern materials are easily used to deliteralize or even retract apparent architectural statements.

When Louis Kahn designs a museum, a similar emptying out occurs. These are sacred spaces for supra-earthly contemplation, where light is treated as a mystical presence or supernatural visitor, providing a model of what human users might aspire to. Thus the roof structure becomes an element of utmost moment and often remains unsettled and subject to change until late in the process.

This could be read as an allegory—the roof is the building's link with heaven or the membrane between the building and the heavens. At the Yale Center for British Art, a web of sloping concrete beams which diffuse light from above aren't so far from Terragni's glass framework which only suggests a roof. Kahn's courtyard feels neither indoor nor outdoor. Its walls are perforated with "windows" and made of concrete and oak, the one a bony masonry, the other a satiny flesh.

One of his most persistent aims is to bring out the expressive potential, even the inherent spirituality, of concrete. At another museum, in Fort Worth, Kahn makes the plot feel like a thinly disguised Greek temple site. Materials this time are travertine and concrete, like semi-ruined and fresh states of the same substance. Once again Kahn shows that a ritualized, even a benighted conception of the role of architecture is compatible with modernist forms and materials. Although he also designed churches and synagogues, Kahn is most interesting for extending the territory of the sacred by approaching museums, libraries, and seats of government as numinous or sacred places. At least the first of these building types has been permanently deflected toward the sacred by his practice.

Kahn redirects secular commissions toward the sacred; contrarily there have always been those who pervert sacred commissions toward a style of play or invention which has little to do with religion. Among the most extravagant is Philibert de l'Orme's chapel at Anet, the coffering of whose dome is generated by rotating an ellipse from a fixed point in the lantern and realizing this graphic riddle in three dimensions.

In a much more thoroughgoing way than de l'Orme, Piranesi is an architect turned graphic designer, assembler of fragments not wholes. His single realized architectural commission is a church for the Knights of Malta which culminates in a high altar like an exploding chimneypiece or sarcophagus, composed of ridged, fluted, and frilled chunks which seem to jostle for a place when there isn't room for all of them. The whole building is a solid block on which time has engraved crude overlapping messages like a rich dilettante's archaeological collection, and constitutes an essay in the heaviness of spiritual material.

Piranesi seems thoroughly profane, unless tombs inevitably lead one away from the mundane and the here and now. To write a complete history of the spread of a denuminized view one would need to look at the secularization of religious themes in nineteenth- century painting via anthropological accuracy and psychological realism. D. G. Rossetti's *Annunciation* is a striking example of the latter which interprets the meeting of the angel and the virgin in sexual terms. She is a terrified innocent in her celibate's cell; he effeminate, half unclothed, the agent of a force seen also in the room's upright, pronged furniture. The vision calls for a psychoanalyst not a priest to draw out its implications.

At the Sacred Heart church in Prague by Jože Plečnik, an inventive but decadent Slovenian designer who also made subtle improvements at Prague Castle, the narrative is less obvious but just as subversive. His church teems with the most varied play, whose sources are hard to trace. A squat Doric temple has been perched atop a windowless rampart-base like an Egyptian tomb. The battered tower has strayed from an Egyptian temple too. Only because a certain amount of Christian imagery is tagged onto the building's surface and its skyline do we recognize this as a church at all.

Finally, the most devastating contradiction—inside the tower you find a modernist betrayer at the heart of the building. It is a large anti-Christian void painted white and filled by a ramp passing up between glazed clock faces, which create a light-filled Corbusian space where conventionally you might expect to find the mechanism of bells or clock. Here only the most exhilarating emptiness, under the circumstances a studied antispiritual effect.

No one has accused Le Corbusier at Ronchamp of that particular crime. On the contrary, followers have expressed disappointment that he seems to have given in to irrational forces. Looking at the plan, experiencing the interior, it is hard not to agree that this nonbeliever has sought an analogue to religious experience in mental disorder and subversion of normal logic. The result is an exciting disorientation which is too easily traced to the designer's willfulness.

It is a common pattern. The most interesting modern brushes with the sacred seem deflective if not positively undermining. Like Monet's extended study of Rouen cathedral which no one could accuse of frivolity, they turn acts of devotion into scientific experiments and redirect attention from the underlying nature of reality to an artistic problem preoccupying the producer.

9

Subjectivity

Subjectivity is hard to define. Ordinarily it is seen as unarguable, untestable, and thoroughly inconsistent, because bound up with individuality and selfhood. In architecture you might expect it to take the form of flimsy, nonrational structures of exaggerated proportions and uncertain extent. So we would look for buildings gnarled like inner experience; unreliable, even vanishing, like thoughts.

If one starts with the most willful and private cases—though neither of these qualities is an inevitable accompaniment of intense subjectivity—one occasionally finds even there a paradoxical reasonableness. So in the remarkable house built over a period of thirty-five years by Fred Burns in Belfast, Maine, and since demolished, we recognize immediately the sources on which he drew, not the deepest reaches of the imagination but the scrap heap and the dump, for this concoction which asserts so strongly its owner's unlikeness to everyone else is made of found bits, driftwood, and castoffs including decorative frills from demolished or abandoned buildings. Even the most characteristic feature of all, the unpredictable color scheme, is probably so lively for the same reason a patchwork quilt is—he couldn't salvage much of any single color.

One of the temptations this house offers is trying to reconstruct the process by which it arose. Like other such artifacts it probably underwent metamorphic revision, and older bits did not stay the same for long. Even within this fluid evolution it is more regular than it looks at first. A wild idea, repeated or expanded, becomes a convention. So the first set of horizontal battens turned a bit of wall into ridges of a reptile's skin. But by the time this treatment has spread over most of the fabric it has become a system, however bizarre, and now a spectator can become used to it.

Freakish constructs like the Burns house are more often spoken into the void than propounded in the heart of established cities. The ones which keep proliferating in an ad hoc way, like the

House of the Winds in Thunder Mountain, Nevada, are often try-ing to impose some kind of personality on a fairly blank slate. This maker is driven by the surrounding desert (as others by the anonymity of the suburbs) to embellish a preexisting structure. As at Gehry's house in Santa Monica, underneath an elaborate cam-ouflage subsists a piece of ordinary vernacular building, in the case of Thunder Mountain a log cabin. It is posted with inscriptions, hung with carved and molded figure sculptures, and amplified by a wiry skeleton which looks like the outlines of walls and par-titions except that all the struts are the arms and legs, the bows, arrows, and rifles of emaciated figures—Indians and settlers per-forming a comic book version of local history. Though exuberant to the verge of madness, it is also rigid like madness and shows no sign of coming to an end. Past efforts seem to spur the cre-ator to pointless repetitions, a sequence which may not be so re-mote from the processes of high art, in the whole career if not in the single work.

The related problem of creativity running out of control (as against coldly flaying itself to further production) is as likely to be met in such home-made works of architecture as anywhere on earth. At the J. Pullam house in North Carolina vehicles and bits of vehicles appear unexpectedly in the higher reaches. In this work cannibalized pieces of other things haven't lost their original iden-tities: windows and even dormers from other buildings have been hastily tacked on. Indoor and outdoor have somewhat broken down: "porches" are just rooms lacking one or two of their walls and stuffed so thickly with a collection of objects that it looks like storage.

Finally the individuality of the project inheres in its lack of sys-tem, even in how it neglects to use the bits collected and lets them silt up deeper and deeper round it. At any moment you come, the building will look incomplete and you might conclude that it is being taken apart. Pullam's house suggests a shifting, precarious process held together or kept up by its associated debris, flexible like consciousness and without identifiable destination. One finally doubts whether habitable space is the primary goal or whether the incomplete illusion of space and house may not be enough.

If you said to the fabricator of the Pullam house that he had made an ultramodernist work he wouldn't know what you were talking about. Yet the formal similarities with a hypersophisticated piece like Kurt Schwitters's Hannover *Merzbau* are overwhelming. The *Merzbau* doesn't spill out into the landscape trailing debris like a mound of refuse, but is fitted—if preposterously: a few floors have been punctured or knocked out—into an existing interior. It began as an ungainly sculpture, perhaps unconsciously modeled on the plague columns familiar in various East European towns, teetery ascents to heaven with odd saints and putti glued to them at various points along the way. Before long Schwitters's towerlet grew to the walls in search of support like a parasitic vine, attaching itself by a webbing that became more solid in stages, progressing from rope and wire to wood and plaster.

Eventually it took over the space, crowding out the possibility of other uses. In the end it included more than forty grottoes, each with its relic or object of veneration. Schwitters's urine in one, Goethe's leg in another, a piece of women's underwear left behind by the owner or filched by Schwitters, Moholy-Nagy's sock, and many others.

Schwitters has been castigated for a fundamental lack of seriousness in the project by those who, like all of us now after the *Merzbau*'s destruction in the war, know it only from photographs (from which it has now been partly reconstructed in the Hannover museum). Like the amateur assemblages, it was made of junk and grew in ways undoubtedly not foreseen from very far off. But unlike J. Pullam or Fred Burns, Schwitters was a conscious artist and gave all the inconsistency an impartial and deindividualizing coat of white paint, making it into a modernist building gone wrong. Finally its claim on us is that of a supremely uneasy work, nervously proliferating, until there are too many ideas in too small a space, too many buildings in what is really no-space. Like the amateur builders Schwitters has been carried away by his idea and has built a city or the Tower of Babel, the final all-inclusive construction, indoors. To enjoy it one must suspend or even countermand most of what one expects from architecture.

The *Merzbau* is a late and eccentric example of a nineteenth-century genre, the artist's own house, which is founded on the idea that a house can represent the self. Dozens or even hundreds of these freaks exist, like the sculptor Bilek's in Prague, which doesn't look much like a house, but that is the point. The whole thing is a fragment expressively broken off and otherwise rough-hewn, like an incompletely carved block which is becoming one of his own tormented sculptures. Bilek, a particular favorite of Kafka's, produces figures reaching or craning toward something you can't see or define, so that they are energetic and undecided at the same time.

His house echoes these disproportions: the top story is compressed as by a weight, and massive concrete columns form a cage for the carved brick facade. Like his works in wood the house resembles a gnarled growth found deep in the forest, faintly archaic and above all grotesque.

Inevitably there are paradoxes in the idea of architecture expressing purely personal meanings. One of the ancestors of such willful and eccentric buildings was Fonthill Abbey, to which William Beckford retired to live down the disgrace of unorthodox sexual behavior. So here was a monastery for a single monk hidden deep in the Wiltshire countryside, but advertising itself with an enormous spindly tower, the whole more imposing in its proportions than many medieval abbeys. This mock-religious building expressed Beckford not in detail but in scale and perversion: strange new uses to which old forms are put individualize them, somewhat as the poet Pope individualized heroic conventions by satirizing them. Thus the pasticheur or chameleon comes to seem an original, and thus endless and pompous spaces acquire a romantic edge.

One of the most impressive interiors in the Abbey was an octagon, modeled on Ely's but much taller, with so called nunneries (where virgins were deflowered?) in a gallery under the roof. Surprisingly often, high narrow tubes of space turn up as the culmination of intense nonrational architectural thinking, as also at Behrens's dye works for Hoechst of ca. 1920, or in the house Melnikov built for himself in late-1920s Moscow. This consists of two tubes, a public and a private one, interlocking, the difference signaled by different fenestration.

The rear cylinder which contains the studio and sleeping room is lit by prismatic openings which from outside appear to violate conventional story and room divisions. Like other of this architect's wild ideas, this was technically well within the capacity of ordinary bricklayers, but the final coats of rendering gave it a phantasmagoric look, like the eyes of monsters in dreams.

Melnikov had strange theories about sleep, believing that dreams could be passed between sleepers if they were not physically impeded, so he ruled out separate bedrooms and arranged all the beds on sloping stone pedestals with only screens or baffles separating them. Subjectivity was a large, not to be neglected preserve in which there was a brisk trade at night.

In ultrasubjective dwellings, beds and bedrooms are often a particular focus. In the bedroom William Burges designed for himself, dreams are already depicted in a cacophonous variety of mediums. When described it sounds painfully literal, but in fact the hubbub works just because of the relentless overlay of one thing on another. The painted and carved stories, all in some sense borrowed, when combined become his.

A later obsessive character, Simon Rodia, worked outdoors and created one of the great monuments to a subjective vision in borrowed forms and materials, which has been rather obtusely linked by scholars to festive constructions in his native Italy. Like Beckford's his towers are unashamedly jerrybuilt, an intrinsic part of their phantasmagoric character. All the diverse surfaces are covered with found objects stuck in the rendering or impressed on it and then removed. Patterns made by accumulations of glazed tile fragments, seashells, slag, bottle bottoms, fractured drainpipes, outlines of tools used in building the whole, and much else only exist by virtue of what Rodia was able to find, hauling his salvage back at weekends on foot and by streetcar.

After his construction became semi-famous he refused to talk about what it meant, unlike many other verbose makers of such artifacts. It was like a front porch exfoliating from his house on a triangular plot next to a railroad right of way, an alternative house or house of dreams next door. But when his house burnt down Rodia left the towers behind and never wanted to return or hear about their fate.

Not all phantasmagoric constructions are so idiosyncratic. One of the most sophisticated is the system of towers and pavilions erected to accommodate royal festivals and marriages at the Zwinger in Dresden. The Kronentor resembles an oversized object from outside architecture which has become a powerful hallucination—a great crown has settled on a semitransparent wall and now constitutes a gate. Thus it qualifies as subjective, that is, engaging deep levels of experience, and not just fanciful.

The wall which unites all the separate episodes often breaks open at just the points where it seems most solid. Next comes the

Wallpavillon, an uneasy idea gracefully carried out, a small building straddling or implanted in the wall, where the windows in the colonnade jump up a story like a hitch in the stride. In the throng of oversized objects this one is a jewel casket, dotted with half-figures turning to froth and making a surface agitation, in the spirit of thought so wayward it breaks all the rules.

A twentieth-century translation of the faceted pavilion appeared in 1914 at the Werkbund Exhibition in Cologne—Bruno Taut's Glass Pavilion. Here subjective expression inheres in materials and structural forms, not in explicit imagery like the figures and urns on the Zwinger. Somehow it was more acceptable and abstemious to decorate the structure with large uplifting inscriptions than to adorn it with figural sculpture. But to Taut and his friends glass had come to possess spiritual properties, and glass stairs between walls of glass under a glass dome expressed a psychic ascent or progress.

Taut's curves are bounded and complete. In Le Corbusier's Maison La Roche the large studio-gallery space has a curved front wall; on its inside surface rises a ramp which follows the curve. Unlike Taut's tight spiral this represents an escape from bounds, a way of thinking beyond the limits of the room and projecting the subject into a kind of landscape transcending the normal restrictions of closed domestic arrangements.

A related spiral is the generating force in Bruce Goff's most extravagant project. Not financially extravagant: the Bavinger house was virtually self-build. It is another artist's house and offered an escape from many of the constraints of ordinary life. Its route to freedom led away from rooms and stories. Along a continuous rising path pods are thrown out and life occurs in these intermediate areas, none of them exactly closed, no internal walls and no ceilings, only the untrimmed exterior skin of found stone and glass slag, between which and the spiral metal roof is a continuous glazed opening. Likewise the entrance is a glass slice through the spiral, trying to pretend there are no other boundaries.

In this building the spiral carries an even heavier ideological burden than in Taut and Corb. The fabric and the life it contains are conceived as seamless wholes, but with stopping places and a new rigidity of circulation: there is only one route and a fixed sequence. Goff's design has picked up the nickname Snail House, which reminds us of a particular source in the natural world. It is also a model of consciousness as fundamentally unstructured. Yet the awkward necessity of the stopping places along the way suggests that our life isn't fully fluid, only intermittently, and that it needs rigid boundaries too. In short the idea of the continuum fits only limited aspects of consciousness.

A more modest attempt to insist on continuities rather than divisions is seen in the curves Haring and Scharoun impart to the facades of their housing blocks at Siemenstadt in Berlin. These are the balconies, which in Scharoun's case blur the boundaries between flats. Coming on them in the present context points up a paradox in designs which seem to take the individuality of the client into account, when the architect cannot know who the client is. Needs which feel very personal to the user turn out to be generic and widely shared, in this case a liking for unruly variation and spaces of peculiar, nonrectilinear shape.

For complication of overlapping curves, one of Borromini's Roman facades like the Propaganda Fide (typically a Counter-Reformation institution) makes almost anything else look quiet. Yet we may doubt whether this pronounced agitation is either personal or subjective. The design is perhaps too intellectual to merit that description, and it is an institutional commission, yet some of the awkward or at least unexpected juxtapositions seem to be passionate statements, uttered with intensity. Borromini uses concepts, intellectual elements, to surprise and unsettle the viewer, instilling his own precarious sort of consciousness. It is a lesson often repeated on this facade, as in a convex window frame which bulges out just under a concave cornice.

This window frame is one of a set of miniature architectural compositions, one per story in vertical series in the center of the facade. Each is crowned by a different "pediment" which erupts with cool violence while staying within the bounds of its quadrant in the subliminal grid. Borromini's imagery too is marked by controlled intensity. Its subjects are not arresting in themselves—palm leaves, crowns, stars—but the sharpness of depiction gives them hallucinatory claims on our attention. How do we know that they stand for suffering, these innocent objects? And if martyrdom is the subject, how odd to find the architect so fully acquainted with it.

The present colors of the Propaganda's main portal (pink, purplish gray, and salmon) are visceral, not architectural, and the forms—curves turning themselves inside out—suggest painful bodily movement, joints turned backward until they crack. Wherever they derive from, these complications are elevated here into spiritual anguish, and thus Borromini's most intimate sensations are able to take shelter under religion.

His drawings often illuminate the relation between subjective experience and articulate cultural forms. Studies for the Oratory of the Filippini show him thinking in knots or nodes of energy, temporarily forgetting the underlying structural system and producing a ghostly figment or mirage, an impression enhanced by the convention of drawing only one half of a symmetrical whole.

Here the entablature grows to disturbing dimensions while reminding us of its humble origins: this architect's aberrations are always recognizable as deviants from a simple norm. It is a subjectivity which expresses itself in hard edges and clear forms, which has distilled its unorthodox longings to piercingly graspable form.

In his most concentrated work, the university church of S. Ivo, the building is first seen trapped in the surrounding fabric of the city, its tower an alien being glimpsed over rooftops and then its body confined between the sides of a skinny court. This is a variant of the perspective gallery at Palazzo Spada, a little joke on perception which uses unexpected shrinkage to embarrass the spectator with his or her own physical grossness.

S. Ivo is wedged into the end of a vista, its situation dictated by conditions which preceded it. So, inside, it explodes upward, the direction in which one will have to look for freedom. The space undergoes a strange metamorphosis, exfoliating as star, circle, flower—all compressed central forms. Here again an overpowering entablature shapes our spatial sensations, crimping and reworking the simple volume of the dome until it becomes intricate and hard to grasp, something of psychological significance above all, the ultimate lesson in Borromini's fusing of the unspeakably personal with the mathematically precise.

More violent disruptions of safe architectural norms exist, of course. At Giulio Romano's Palazzo Te in Mantua small architectural incidents met outside prepare one, but inadequately, for the turmoil of the Room of the Giants. These initial signs consist of such things as dropped triglyphs and erratic intercolumniation; among the giants deviations are more extreme, but in the form of painted murals rather than solid architectural confusion. Instead of constructing a building in the process of collapse and letting spectators make what they would of it, Giulio has narrated such an event, showing its cause and its parallel in the world of human bodies, so we have giants falling and crushed under architectural orders which are coming apart. It is perhaps not as clownishly literal as may appear: an attack on stability mounted by someone who understands where feelings of safety within walls and under roofs come from. Finally the exercise manipulates our subjective experience of space: the ultimate object of this demonstration is the spectator, who is to realize intimately what it is to mistrust a building when deep inside it.

A subtler version of subjective space in painting, again obtained by measuring an outburst of disruptive energy against a stable architectural background, is found in El Greco's *Moneychangers*. It brings certain architectural constants over into the human realm—the ideas of uprights and of recession—and it shows reality blown about by winds or consumed like flames.

Many examples can be found in his work of the exaggerated division between earthbound and skyward evident in *The Burial of the Count of Orgaz*, which skews the boring symmetry familiar in most pictures that show heaven and earth together by displacing the weight in the human sector to the left. Doubtless El Greco would not accept "subjective" as the name for the skyward tendency. Yet his world is organized not by ordinary laws of physics but by powers of wish or thought. It encourages us to think that we can override (albeit by strenuous application) aspects of reality which don't fit with our vision of it.

In the extravagant late Baroque facades of the Portuguese architect Soares da Silva the shapes of formerly recognizable organizing motifs are lost. Lintels, door frames, pediments, cornices: they spread out like regular ripples in a pool, becoming Blakean emanations which before long collide with other elements to which they adhere. Although the mode of development or increase is fairly systematic, the result is not mainly decorative but resembles a reality like El Greco's full of sudden flarings or eruptions. Although the whole is roughly symmetrical, this consistency is undone by shadows which differentiate similar elements. Getting back to the simple classical constituents would be an artificial enterprise, for moldings have melted and deformed past hope of recovery. It is a world controlled by the power of feeling, in which geometry exists only to be violated and the more stable parts take their meaning from the more abandoned.

This composition encourages if it doesn't compel you to adopt strange perspectives, to focus obsessively on parts at the expense of the whole, to seek out viewpoints which produce maximum distortion, or best of all to string these together in unrepeatable sequences. Then the stone becomes truly molten and adjacent motifs loom larger or disappear entirely in momentous dramas staged by the whims of our movement. Such excitements are impossible to keep track of and such buildings will not be the same twice.

More dispersed compositions might be thought to make such perspectivism easier. The Charles Bridge in Prague was transformed into an architectural landscape by the addition of Baroque sculpture to the late Gothic base. Most of these are multiple figure groups in stepped series. They barely hang together and at times it seems futile even to try to make a coordinated progress out of this long trek. Repeatedly one comes within the force field of the next sculpted group and is active all over again watching them form and reform, played against the faster movements of passersby. The histrionic gestures of these saints do not pick up further meanings as one circles round, but are like shadow animals projected on blank walls, or flickering angel limbs in Tiepolo, caused by practically involuntary spasms of the brush. There is a primitive subjectivity which though extremely pure travels along the surface.

Certain Mannerist paintings provide earlier examples of dispersed architectural compositions as potentially subjective. Antoine Caron's *Augustus and the Sybil* shows ancient Rome as a wide paved plane. Scattered across this largely empty landscape, like a forecast of Tschumi's La Villette, are a collection of nearly useless monumental structures, all different, all frill, not triumphal arches but triumphal gazebos. Crowds of small figures are dotted and then bunched around them in apparently irrational fashion. The only way to visit these high spots would be a zigzag course, a real vagary. This awkward composition sets going the most willful movement, the perceiver turned loose to create the world by assembling sensations in an unforeseeable series.

Among experiments with autonomy for the parts in an architectural composition, a facade project of 1571 by the Swiss designer Hans Bock the Elder ranks high, like a Piranesi prison introduced into a solid bourgeois street. Single windows with their framing pilasters lurch forward to form an advance guard for a structure which largely lags three layers further back. Or they form the crowning stage in a precarious pile narrowing toward the top. Holes are punched out, gangways run between, carved putti lose their footing: the result is like something thrown badly out of line, though not toppled, by an earthquake. The saving or damning proviso is that this was only intended as a trompe-l'oeil painting on a conventional flat facade.

Only in the twentieth century would it become culturally feasible actually to build such disorderly imagining into permanence. If we were writing the history of architectural extravagance perhaps we would need to think harder about the sensations inspired in contemporary viewers (supposing this project had been carried out). Perhaps it didn't discharge but only aggravated their need to see such subversions made three-dimensional.

Czech Cubism is one of the earliest and in some ways most flagrant of twentieth-century attacks on architectural stability. In its most exciting moments hardly an inch of the fabric holds still. We have entered a world, like some fairground prank with mirrors, without a truly flat surface anywhere. So the entrance of Josef Chochol's flats on Neklanova in Prague with its appended prismatic porch induces something akin to paranoia. For us there can be no rest or relaxation but a kind of mental circling like that of a bird looking unsuccessfully for a perch. Finally of course this design raises the doubt brought on by any building which tries to enshrine a moment of crisis: will one's identity continue susceptible under its methodical attack, or will one begin to find its terrible uncertainty diverting? However Kafkaesque its beginnings, this mode too evolved before long into a set of conventions. Kafka himself, come to that, is a very literary writer who uses old tale patterns to pose insoluble riddles.

Expressionist film sets have the advantage in this context of being in a special way temporary architecture, experienced once and then swallowed by succeeding frames. So in *The Cabinet of Dr. Caligari* streets and buildings take sudden bends according to a flamboyant but relatively simple code: emotion is expressed as sharp angles and careening diagonals along which creep crooked figures clothed in black.

At least once Le Corbusier creates a subjective space like a stage set or a painting, classical not expressionist, on the rooftop of the Beistegui apartment off the Champs-Elysées. It offers, instead of views of Paris, Surrealist hallucinations of selected monuments peering over the shrubbery. Like De Chirico's pictures these spaces provoke a question: are they artificial inventions or true plumbings of the subconscious, are they superficial or deep?

Le Corbusier's "garden" makes us reflect on the displaced logic of all his other roof gardens, never more than when we climb to the final raised, roofless room, paved with grass and furnished with a rococo chimneypiece connected to no chimney. This is a setting for psychodrama, a place where functional appliances are deprived of function, strangely akin to the world of Duchamp's urinal. The culmination is a true nowhere, an enigma whose content we must supply or lack. The most complete subjectivity remains a blank.

10
Memory

Adolf Loos limited architecture strictly speaking to the monument and the tomb, considering all other structures constrained, sullied, even defiled by use. Of course he was pulling the rug out from under architecture as much as he was dignifying tombs. The memorial function isn't really central in what buildings do, at least if one means their ability to record an affect, after the actuality of which the building preserves the memory has disappeared.

This conscious striving for permanence is the main subject here, as well as some cases of permanence unsought, where accident makes a particular structure the last or nearly the last of its type. When its proper use is discontinued and half forgotten, the building remains to remind the serious student, who learns to read the signs it preserves, of vanished customs or ways of life.

When Loos came to design a tomb for the art historian Max Dvořak he attempted an anti-architectural statement but found himself hemmed in by some of the simplest properties of matter. He was trying to render a void in circumscribed form, for which he chose black stone in primitive masonry of large blocks. The form is that of a house but of such reduced dimensions that it becomes notional, like a sentry box. Instead of a gable this cube of stone is topped off with a stylized rendition of the grave mound, a stepped ziggurat familiar in other Loos works like the tomblike department store intended for Alexandria.

As the Dvořak tomb was never built and never covered internally with the Kokoschka frescoes projected, we can't be entirely sure whether the blackness would have stopped at a skin of black marble or been carried through in granite or tufa. How culturally local is black, anyway, as the sign for nothing or for death as an end? How unmistakable is the zigzag roof as a sign for the grave which lies underneath and is not this time literally mounded up, a bulge which signifies and *is* in its miserable way the person gone underground?

Loos's design is minimal and elegant at once, its lack of ornament best appreciated by a student of ornament like Dvořak. Loos is after all the architect who never forgot that a designer's rooms would eventually be spaces people died in, and in this perspective most of the vagaries of sophisticated decor seemed to him intolerable. Yet such thinking is the moment of death seen by the fully sentient outsider; the dying person isn't likely to care about such fitness. Besides which, most inhabitants will not want to strip their houses in advance to get the right setting for the last act of the drama.

In his struggle to find something worthy of the reality he was called on to represent in this tomb, Loos harks back to the neolithic ancestors of most monuments in modern cemeteries. In their present denuded state these stone cairns, which are most plentiful in the uninhabited hill regions of Britain, have a heroic gauntness which would have pleased him. They provide a crevice to lodge in—the contents long since pilfered—and a covering, usually the most impressive element, a large flat stone which may be fallen or reerected to form a roof over the cavity. Originally these bony members didn't show themselves but were covered with a soft mound of earth. When the cairn's present state is disheveled enough one can doubt whether it is there at all; accidental groupings in the surrounding rocks seem just about as purposive.

A special little house for the dead is one of the most persistent forms for the memorial, sometimes open as if it crystallizes a canopy raised temporarily during the interment ceremony. The Ricketts tomb at Kensal Green by William Burges multiplies all the elements of such a construction while clasping tightly to the casket within. It incorporates eight gables and eight columns supporting them, which almost touch a further eight holding up the sarcophagus, a structure within a structure. The whole is capped by fat finials and cusps like nodding reptile heads. Superfluity or excessive provision is the underlying idea: at the moment when a person no longer needs shelter you are extra careful to provide it. In this way architecture invariably becomes unreal, a kind of mock-building, in the presence of death.

Even more hypothetical are the houses for donors' remains inside the churches built largely to contain them and to provide a setting for masses for the repose of their souls. One of the most elaborate donor's tombs commemorates Margaret of Austria at Brou. It consists of arches which look like magnificent portals but lead only to an image of the prostrate corpse. They are crowned with extravagant parapets which take their places under the much less elaborate roof of the sponsoring building. The tomb is not to be outdone by its larger casing. Like many images of its century, Margaret's effigy lies atop another layer of depiction. In a darker arcaded space just beneath we find her skeleton in sculpted form, a further version, more real and piercing, of the same thing.

At another extreme are the miniature buildings in which the eighteenth century represented death or a specific dead person by means of elemental geometry. These cubes, cylinders, and cones express the irreducible nature of this reality and leave no room for personal reminiscence. Robert Adam gives the genre an extra, undermining twist in his tomb for David Hume in Edinburgh, which consists of a large cylinder heroically rusticated. The entrance to this, for it seems you can enter it, is placed under a smaller representation of the cylinder, an urn in a cylindrical niche. So the monument refers backward to itself: the larger cylinder is really an urn, and the smaller one inset in its front a picture of its parent. Doubling the closed and sealed idea, Adam makes us feel this is a death which will not be undone.

In Boullée's proposal for a giant truncated pyramid, a model is again contained within the larger body. This time it is a temple portico which inhabits a little cavelike crevice at the base with the whole weight of the pyramid bearing down on top of it. The pyramid's chopped-off top makes this monument look industrial, perhaps a furnace, or incomplete.

Boullée had preposterous ideas of filling this with great hollow spaces domed like the Pantheon and occupied by robed figures tending smoking altars. His Egyptian sources, by contrast, have long stood as the most grandiose instances of nearly useless and unused constructions, containing little habitable space. Most of them were robbed early in their life and then no longer contained even that flimsy excuse for existing. But to later generations such absence of function did not weaken their force, and the pyramids represent memories strong if unclear.

They have had many descendants. One of the most surprising is the tomb proposed for Lenin by the Dutch architect Berlage, a lifelong socialist. It would have been a ghoulish fate for this ruler, viewed by the architect as a liberator, to be set off Pharaoh-like in this concentric space with a great weight of coffered masonry pressing down from above and hollowing out the depression in which he is sunk. Lenin did in fact become a relic and his corpse a spectacle, which was not survival in any meaningful sense but a final conversion to pure symbol.

Like Lenin Egyptian mummies were carefully preserved, but they were not like him publicly displayed. There are various precedents for Lenin's exposure, like uncorrupted saints or Snow White, and in Scotland, a tale-infested place, the husband's heart carried round from place to place until the wife joined it in a common grave in an institution named for it, Sweetheart Abbey in Galloway. The corpse (or part of it) resembles architecture in its inertia, which is then capitalized with pedestals or casings and so permanence is extracted from a person's passing.

Corpses may seem an odd inspiration for architecture but they are a common one, sometimes as cues, sometimes as models. A representation of the dead person is a common feature of tombs, even if the extreme materialism of the Lenin memorial is rare, and so we are only reminded of the corpse, not actually confronted with it. On Elizabethan tombs the loneliest experience of all is represented as communal: the most frequent ratio is a husband between two wives, not that they all died together or were this age when they did. They usually occur in an in-between state, not sleeping but laid out in their best clothes, in worldly defiance of death.

The truly prone type is gradually replaced by the lounger, reading a book or staring into space. This posture, derived from classical models where it represents someone attending a banquet, resurfaces for the humanist scholars of Italy. It aims to show the dead person at something like his best, in a pose he assumed more often than the deathbed clinch. So it tries to be about life rather than death, not pure denial but redressing the proportions usually conveyed by tombs.

These meditative figures are succeeded by even less deathbound effigies, strutting types with no unhappiness clinging to them, which come into their own in the late seventeenth and early eighteenth centuries. Such memorials often condense the generations and put forward a family's greatness, something death cannot dent, though it tramples individuals. Some will view this attitude as bravery against the odds, while others will regard it as one of the hollowest displays of human boasting.

As in other realms and forms, the nineteenth century reverts to something somberer. Bilek's *Sorrow* of 1908–1909 in Vysehrad cemetery, Prague, is retrograde for its date. In place of a portrait of the deceased, it puts a soulful allegorical figure like a plume of smoke emitted from the pyre which suggests emotions twisting in their struggle to find release in tolerable form. Death is a subjective, not easily communicable agony, in the face of which pious conventions provide small consolation.

At the other extreme are coercive public symbols visible in famous photographs of a Moscow sculpture yard in the 1930s. Whole rows of Lenins bent over pondering and Stalins looking resolutely into the future fill the space. Lenin and Stalin have been converted to public symbols who strike well-known poses and elicit ritual responses verging on devotion. To understand such monuments fully we must imagine them colonizing the public space of cities, until any walk through the streets becomes a tour of shrines and citizens' movements are slowed, solemnized, made torpid by this official structuring of memory.

Less momentous forms of the urge to commemorate may, like these sinister manifestations, illuminate the whole phenomenon of the memorial. At the bottom of the cascade in the garden at Rousham, an inscribed plaque is inset which remembers a hunting dog whose effects used to be widely felt in the vicinity, at least among the grouse and rabbits who scattered in terror before this bigger-than-average hound. Like Pope's mock-heroic epics this makes a shrunken, telescoped link with a grander past in another place.

The way the contemporary artist Robert Cumming found of commemorating his own recent past could also be described as mock-heroic. Over his bathroom sink in the position of a shaving mirror is a photo of another more decrepit bathroom sink. Above the sink in the photo is another photo of an earlier sink, and so on in a vista which stretches back through the last five places Cumming has lived in his migration through this part of California. It is an absurd but visionary work. Who would bother to record such trivia? And yet these scenes carry surprising weight: we are usually alone when we stop in front of a bathroom mirror and it is a not inappropriate spot in which to dream about the changes time has worked. The perspective of sinks is a displaced portrait of the aging face usually seen above them.

Cumming has found a non-self-referential way to memorialize his own intimate past. Richard Long makes art from his casual (and after a while not so casual) walks. *Crossing the Sahara* of 1988 shows a telling absence, the merest trace of passage across the desert in a curving path made by sweeping away the surface pebbles along a narrow thread stretching into the distance. Halfway back there is a clearing, that is, a slightly flatter space big enough for an animal to lie down in. That roughly circular blank is the nearest to a portrait of the maker we are likely to get. It shows practically nothing, yet it constitutes a covertly egoistic work. Every artist's wildest dream is to make others interested in the trivial details of his life, in this case his undramatic encounter with a few clods of earth. Such modest examples tell us how one might go about architecturalizing the most fugitive memories and about the kind of encumbrance one will be left with: it is a propensity which cannot be indulged too often without cost.

Structures are powerful even when there is little content to put in them. Civilizations differ in what they prize most and most want a detailed record of. Japanese culture has institutionalized the observation of nature and given certain rocks of modest dimensions relic status. These usually look quite ordinary to outsiders, like the famous fifteen at Ryoan-ji which constitute an artificial desert or miniature Sahara. Perhaps the huge heraldic emblems in King's College Chapel, Cambridge, are removed from their normal context in reality by a not unrelated process. These roses and portcullises with heavy crowns hovering over them may be oblique like haiku, instead of the absurdly literal signs for the monarch which they at first appear. The flower is held up not as beautiful or perishable but as concentric and focused like a jewel, and the portcullis represents a threshold and unwavering defenses. These commemorations of what is after all just a person (though a king) are becoming abstract, early visual symbols for the nation.

Early Romanticism thirsts after more voluble, fleshed-out emblems of the spirit of the nation, and so identifies it with great men more characterful than monarchs. So Soane's house fills up with shrines to various human achievements not limited to architecture.

The Shakespeare Recess is a strange little space off the stairs, a chapel or tomblike slot virtually unenterable, hence leaning toward the imaginary, a condensed vista covered in pictorial material. Turning a literary figure into a visual phenomenon presents difficulties, especially when, as with this one, you don't know exactly what he looked like. Soane's solution is to find or commission paintings of important moments in the plays, so the characters become monuments and form a little Pantheon.

Later in the nineteenth century as various European peoples woke up to their nationhood they felt a need to depict its founders. So the Millenary Monument in Budapest reaches back into preliterate times to personalize the beginnings of the Hungarian folk. At this point the patriots are in no mood to admit how little is known of early migrations or of how racial groups got where they are. The seven mythical founders come out looking like an opera cast, mainly set off by extreme variegation of exotic headgear.

These are made-up memories which don't quite know where to go: the seven denizens of the steppes are loosely penned in by a blowsy classical colonnade and they circle round a pompous obelisk, not the sort of structure they could have met riding across the Hungarian plain. Yet nothing could be further from the designers' intention than a portrayal of *Barbarians Visiting the Capital.*

One expects such fantastic displays among groups which come late to political independence: no public sculptures representing the Trojan ancestors of the first Britons have yet been erected. Further ironies collect around the monument in Budapest: when it was begun in 1896 the Hungarians chafed under an Austrian yoke; by the time of its completion in 1929 Hungary had been stripped of half its prewar territory for its association with the losing Austrian side. The lost Hungarian cities, now in Slovakia, Romania, and former Yugoslavia, are commemorated by nostalgic murals in Budapest restaurants, a synoptic presentation connected with loss, on the principle of the posthumous memorial.

Immigrants to America experience the loss of national territory in another way. Long after the separation from their native land, the architect Charles Moore attempted to reconstruct or invent a national heritage for the Italians of New Orleans by building them a crash course in Italian architectural history, the Piazza d'Italia. Because his clients have mainly forgotten Italy the project becomes a pompous joke, full of ironies and discontinuities. For the architect at least, the debris of a tradition is more fun than the real thing. Recently this jolly pastiche has suffered strange reverses, become derelict and been partially rehabilitated, stages the original conception certainly did not foresee. Perhaps Moore regarded his rickety and cut-rate construction as a more temporary kind of history.

Brevity of another kind has overtaken a memorial at Prešov in Slovakia built to commemorate a short-lived proletarian uprising earlier in the century, now partially defaced by the removal of its metal inscription, which can still be read via the pattern of holes and stains left by individual letters. It lies in a bleak "square" with a Party building of the early 1950s as backdrop. This Stalinist monolith with its central towerlet like an informer keeping watch has become a kind of relic or memorial too, that is, a reminder of something disowned if not actually dismantled. The monument which fronts it belongs to an embattled class, war monuments making controversial claims, rewriting the story of a battle or pretending that conquered territory is pleased to welcome the conqueror.

In the Prešov memorial a scattering of heavy metal freedom fighters are crucified on a flat wedge of granite plates. This sloping form makes the historical vision into something not quite real, where people's heroes levitate in the memory, surrounded by a heavy mist of unheroic administration. And to read the whole message of the monument one must include the Stalinist backdrop, which effectively dampens current as opposed to historical ardor.

One of the most ambitious recent monuments on conquered territory, the Soviet war memorial in East Berlin, was among the first large construction projects undertaken when the city still lay in ruins. The grandiose conception required a remote park site at Treptow, so in the end the memorial creates its own world in no visible relation to the Germany it is nominally in. Here an elaborate parade of symbols is mounted which seldom match with those next in line. As at Prešov, fragmentary forms loom large, like the pair of huge dipped flags in red marble, so thick they need copper roofs.

The flags are not even recognizable as flags from a distance and look more like rocket launching ramps. At their feet kneel soldiers dwarfed by the towering wedges overhead. Beyond them lies a kind of waste ground, a mass grave laid out as a formal garden and punctuated by marble blocks with battle scenes in relief labeled with sayings picked out in gold, each signed J. V. Stalin.

At the end of the vista atop its cairnlike mound stands a colossal Red Army soldier made from captured German weapons. He wields a sword and carries a young girl who nestles against his fur collar. This is the final supremely ambiguous image which would be barely recognizable to those Germans who had actually encountered members of the Red Army. Antiquated gear and antique chivalrous behavior—it is a strangely retrograde presentation of the historical vanguard, but it is at home among the assorted parts of this memorial, each with its lesson to teach.

In spite of the overload of iconography the message at Treptow is as simple as that of Lutyens's memorial to the Missing of the

Somme, nonfigurative by contrast and just as massive as the Russian one but a meditation on voids, not victory. For visitors to Treptow too the subliminal point conveyed by the scale and inertia of the scattered memorial is the pointlessness of effort.

Perhaps the most frustrated and extreme statements of this kind were made by Aldo Rossi in monuments to the partisans of two small towns in northern Italy. The memorial proposed but not built for Cuneo is an incomplete room, entered from beneath by a narrowing stair which seems to go nowhere but then opens into a windowless, roofless prison, like a work of James Turrell without the color. Taking away most of the point of architecture, Rossi turns it into a philosophical problem.

In the memorial built at Segrate the idea of the roof is again the pivot on which everything turns. Here gable and roof become a geometrical solid which slides away from the building until almost free and held up by one squat column. In both projects Rossi combines sensations of emptiness and oppressive mass, that is to say positive and negative voids.

What Rossi sees as emptiness, others have tried to see as fullness: at the other extreme from the memorial at Cuneo are crowded, rich textured visions of decay, like an eighteenth-century Italian stage set which depicts one of the parallel cities of tombs which will eventually swallow living cities. This is a claustrophobic vision: finally there will be no space left, as debris accumulates around Doric columns thicker than the spaces between them.

A strange ruin room built in an existing monastery by the late eighteenth-century French architect Charles-Louis Clérisseau is the ultimate colonization of ordinary life by such a vision. Here every appliance is the broken wreck of another, earlier form. All of them, and we too, are being slowly pulverized, to end as dust. Living in a ruin feeds a certain psychology. Does the inhabitant of the fragment see it mainly as a remnant or mainly as an intimation of something gigantic?

One of the most interesting recent efforts to inhabit a ruin turned a forbidding fortress into a museum. When Carlo Scarpa converted the Castelvecchio in Verona he made no stylistic concession to his mentor the past, but he still fitted himself ingeniously into the crevices like those clever parasites who reuse arrangements built with different intentions. Ours is not a heroic age but picks up fallen pieces or gives amusing twists to what already exists. The architectural scenery contrived by Scarpa for displaying the past gets much of its power from feeling abandoned in spite of tentative signs of resuscitation.

Ruins used to scenic effect turn up in surprising places. In the center of a 1960s housing project by Alison and Peter Smithson rise three unequal mounds like prehistoric tumuli. They are actual and not make-believe graves, being built of the rubble of Victorian slums torn down to make way for the Smithson blocks with their "streets in the sky" dangling the loose ends of nonexistent new social nexuses. Future archaeologists may want to dig up the little artificial hills, but in the meantime they function as a children's playground. It is an eighteenth-century idea, to turn a cemetery into a park and to make the presence of the dead less insistent, as if culture belonged to the cycle of the seasons.

Historical revivals in architecture gained momentum in the eighteenth century too, but seem to have an opposite tendency, and to resurrect not inter the past. Making careful replicas of outmoded structures, the designer appears to resist the passage of time and to imagine he can outwit death. Perhaps therefore we should focus on what happens to present users rather than (as is more usual) on violence done to past eras. The fabricator of historical replicas retreats into times before he was born and makes himself an earlier person. However charming in individual instances, there is something defeatist about this excursion from which in some sense one does not intend to return.

Sometimes revivals admit to deep dissatisfaction with the present, sometimes just to vague hankerings after they are not sure what. No one *remembers* life in a primitive hut, yet Lequeu's drawings of huts and Rousseau's groundless speculations about life in them touch a responsive chord in many, who feel a need to cleanse life of complexity and let themselves believe that in finding their way to this practically empty container they are remembering.

The Manx architect Baillie Scott was chosen to resurrect Romanian folk tradition for the crown princess in a Transylvanian forest hideaway raised on wooden stilts like something in a Russian fairy tale. Folkish here means covered in patterns derived from plants; each room's scheme is based on a single flower. Alcoves are a favorite device—just beyond an inglenook is a raised area behind a railing like a side chapel. Over the arch announcing it, a pseudo-Arthurian inscription about a couple transfixed on a threshold.

Nothing could be further from the spirit of the black house at Arnol in the Hebrides than fancy inscriptions, for this house is that strange animal, a preliterate survival. One enters by ducking under a low lintel, heeding the modern inscriptions warning against this, which have multiplied in response to mishaps. Inside, fumes from an unvented peat fire seem intolerable at first but soon fade like a familiar odor. Smoke swirls slowly in the upper reaches blackening the air and the wooden rafters, something of a mystery on this treeless island.

Thus a name which seemed flat, black house, becomes improbably poetic. But the box beds which line the walls are miserable animal pens, not secret dens; and the consoling patterns with which Baillie Scott laces his walls are entirely lacking here. Later we learn that when last lived in, the house boasted wallpaper reaching halfway up the ceiling and patterned linoleum on the floor. The Ministry of Works has returned the decor to a more primitive state, but the vanished dwellers might feel it is now too like the beast quarters across the central passage. Oddly enough, that part has been improved by the Ministry. Originally roof timbers in the byre were skimped owing to scarcity of wood. Eventually this structural weakness required a series of props which offended purists among the restorers, so they brought the beast roof up to the standard of the human one.

The old village of Arnol forms a string at right angles to the main road where new streetlights, sidewalks, and Plexiglas bus shelters feel very suburban. Lining the old street by contrast are abandoned black houses with tin roofs or none, in all stages of dilapidation. Older islanders express equal horror at the black house and young people's disregard for Gaelic culture. Only anthropologists and tourists can wax enthusiastic over the communal atmosphere and cultural warmth created by the old dwellings.

Now, the single visitable black house is certainly a lesson, but of what? The number of restored black houses appears to be growing slowly. A census might well show that it isn't islanders who live in them. Apparently the revival only began when nothing but derelict examples remained: a census of ruins becomes feasible when there aren't too many of them.

Revivals generally have a social agenda which can be pretty coercive. Norman Shaw's church in the early garden suburb of Bedford Park is a counterexample, a reaction against most Gothic revival. By adding frilly wooden trimmings to the roof—a balustrade like a picket fence and a belfry like a gazebo—he detoxifies and domesticates his Gothic base and gives a light, eighteenth-century flavor to religion.

One of Shaw's near contemporaries, Beresford Pite, seems poles apart in his graphic style if not his architecture. Projects like the

West End Clubhouse of 1882 stir up nightmares of inconsistent textures, as if universal leprosy were a kind of ideal. Though Pite is usually gloomy and Shaw is not, their relation to the past is more similar than first appears. In both, a confusing complexity is our main clue to how much has happened and what a rich inheritance we sit on top of.

There is an institution powerfully symptomatic or expressive of this historical situation, the museum. Museums are warehouses of memories or intellectual graveyards in which there can't be too much, an attitude clearer in connoisseurs' cabinets than in more recent, sparser forms. But emptiness in museums is known all along to be perverse and delusive, a way of keeping memories in check. The most extreme example of such denial is Robert Venturi's skeletal mock-up of Benjamin Franklin's long-disappeared house, executed in steel, a material Franklin could not have used, as if to say history is all made up and we don't really know what the past looks like.

But you only need to be turned loose in the streets of a city like Krakow, the old capital of Poland, to feel the oppressive weight and nearness of the past, vomiting debris into the present, most powerfully when decrepit and tottering toward its fall, when vulnerable and not especially beautiful. There's a whole other subject here of memories not programmatically preserved but elusive and densely overlaid, of many lives which surface momentarily in old paint, obsolete wiring, and forgotten cupboards but are mainly lost.

Afterword

The present book can date itself precisely to a single provocation. Someone I worked with asserted that while she launched ambitious theoretical investigations, I trudged along in circumstantial narrative. I shouldn't have been surprised, for "theory" has been a bit of a bugbear recently, at least in my corner of the world. Theory's antagonist, for want of a better, has been history, depicted as both dull and naive, slow to catch on to the fact that after Derrida (or whoever) there can be no more history, all continuity in thought being hopelessly compromised and reality such a minefield that it allows one only various ways of expressing the inability to take a confident step in any direction.

But what is theory? On the one hand, "theorists" claiming that what they do is distinctive and superior. On the other, little hard evidence to justify the usurpation. I am not a naturally theoretical person, being too focused on the individuality of the objects I have chosen to study. (If there were time I would pick quarrels with every word in that sentence, especially "objects," "chosen," and "study." I could almost as well say they choose me and study me.) Yet I have felt goaded to see if there weren't a way I could practice theory, which would not set itself up as another orthodoxy but lend a kind of validity to the term. To be authentically theoretical, what would that mean? Tackling the largest ideas head-on rather than letting them come up and then shortly disappear in the course of another discussion.

The large ideas of the book were chosen not because they matched each other or led to a goal, but because individually they were the most important I could think of. Every one of them was awkward as much as harmonious; none could be thoroughly digested by architecture. Thus it happened that some were parts of the material of architecture itself, some were allied disciplines, and some were human activities or faculties which architecture gave a home to or had to negotiate with. Lack of congruity among the parts I judged not a serious flaw, or not a flaw at all, because the goal was to reflect comprehensively on the slippery hybrid, architecture, an entity so difficult to pin firmly in place that it needed to be approached from many directions. So the intention was something like a Cubist portrait of a sitter who wouldn't hold still. The goal might be a sense of wholeness but the method would be oblique, starting likely as not in dissimilarity or in surrealist juxtaposition, which besides a point of contact brought out unassimilable difference in the two halves of the comparison.

The book has learned many of its principles of formal organization from poetry, among them a dislike of explanatory justification, and has used the idea of the model as the intellectual pivot on which a great deal turns. All the objects in the book become something like models: they are germs, seeds, or embryos which are capable of magical or mechanical reproduction. Some of the transformations are more lasting than others and the whole experiment shows us more clearly how much of life we can safely turn over to the imagination.

Illustration Credits

Chapter 1 Finca Miralles Gate. Antoni Gaudí. Barcelona, Spain. 1901–1902. Photo: Alan Chandler.

Chapter 2 Origin III. Shin Takamatsu. Kamigyo-ku, Kyoto, Japan. 1986. Photo: Nacása & Partners.

Chapter 3 Ossuary. Sedlec, Bohemia. Frantisek Rint. Ca. 1870. Photo: author.

Chapter 4 French farmhouse. Near Rodez, in the Aveyron. Early eighteenth century. Photo: author.

Chapter 5 Public and Private Buildings Executed by Sir J. Soane between 1780 and 1815. Painting by Joseph Gandy. Photo: A. C. Cooper Ltd. By courtesy of the Trustees of Sir John Soane's Museum, London.

Chapter 6 Cemetery chapel of Sv. Jan Nepomuk. Giovanni Santini. Zdar, Moravia. Begun 1719. Photo: author.

Chapter 7 Latvian Riflemen Memorial. Riga, Latvia. 1969–1970. Photo: author.

Chapter 8 Street shrine. Braga, Portugal. Photo: author.

Chapter 9 Merzbau. Kurt Schwitters. Hannover, Germany. 1933 (destroyed). Photo: Sprengel Museum Hannover.

Chapter 10 Street in Krakow. Photo: author.

Index